"This series is a tremendous resource for tho
understanding of how the gospel is woven ᴜ.
pastors and scholars doing gospel business from all the Scriptures. This is a biblical and theological feast preparing God's people to apply the entire Bible to all of life with heart and mind
wholly committed to Christ's priorities."

> **BRYAN CHAPELL,** President Emeritus, Covenant Theological Seminary; Senior Pastor,
> Grace Presbyterian Church, Peoria, Illinois

"Mark Twain may have smiled when he wrote to a friend, 'I didn't have time to write you a
short letter, so I wrote you a long letter.' But the truth of Twain's remark remains serious and
universal, because well-reasoned, compact writing requires extra time and extra hard work.
And this is what we have in the Crossway Bible study series *Knowing the Bible*. The skilled authors and notable editors provide the contours of each book of the Bible as well as the grand
theological themes that bind them together as one Book. Here, in a 12-week format, are carefully wrought studies that will ignite the mind and the heart."

> **R. KENT HUGHES,** Visiting Professor of Practical Theology, Westminster Theological
> Seminary

"*Knowing the Bible* brings together a gifted team of Bible teachers to produce a high-quality
series of study guides. The coordinated focus of these materials is unique: biblical content,
provocative questions, systematic theology, practical application, and the gospel story of God's
grace presented all the way through Scripture."

> **PHILIP G. RYKEN,** President, Wheaton College

"These *Knowing the Bible* volumes provide a significant and very welcome variation on the
general run of inductive Bible studies. This series provides substantial instruction, as well as
teaching through the very questions that are asked. *Knowing the Bible* then goes even further
by showing how any given text links with the gospel, the whole Bible, and the formation of
theology. I heartily endorse this orientation of individual books to the whole Bible and the
gospel, and I applaud the demonstration that sound theology was not something invented
later by Christians, but is right there in the pages of Scripture."

> **GRAEME L. GOLDSWORTHY,** former lecturer, Moore Theological College; author,
> *According to Plan, Gospel and Kingdom, The Gospel in Revelation*, and *Gospel and Wisdom*

"What a gift to earnest, Bible-loving, Bible-searching believers! The organization and structure
of the Bible study format presented through the *Knowing the Bible* series is so well conceived.
Students of the Word are led to understand the content of passages through perceptive, guided
questions, and they are given rich insights and application all along the way in the brief but
illuminating sections that conclude each study. What potential growth in depth and breadth
of understanding these studies offer! One can only pray that vast numbers of believers will
discover more of God and the beauty of his Word through these rich studies."

> **BRUCE A. WARE,** Professor of Christian Theology, The Southern Baptist Theological
> Seminary

KNOWING THE BIBLE

J. I. Packer, Theological Editor
Dane C. Ortlund, Series Editor
Lane T. Dennis, Executive Editor

•   •   •   •   •   •

Genesis	Psalms	Jonah, Micah, and Nahum	Ephesians
Exodus	Proverbs		Philippians
Leviticus	Ecclesiastes	Haggai, Zechariah, and Malachi	Colossians and Philemon
Numbers	Song of Solomon		
Deuteronomy	Isaiah	Matthew	1–2 Thessalonians
Joshua	Jeremiah	Mark	1–2 Timothy and Titus
Judges	Lamentations, Habakkuk, and Zephaniah	Luke	
Ruth and Esther		John	Hebrews
1–2 Samuel		Acts	James
1–2 Kings	Ezekiel	Romans	1–2 Peter and Jude
1–2 Chronicles	Daniel	1 Corinthians	1–3 John
Ezra and Nehemiah	Hosea	2 Corinthians	Revelation
Job	Joel, Amos, and Obadiah	Galatians	

•   •   •   •   •   •

J. I. PACKER is Board of Governors' Professor of Theology at Regent College (Vancouver, BC). Dr. Packer earned his DPhil at the University of Oxford. He is known and loved worldwide as the author of the best-selling book *Knowing God*, as well as many other titles on theology and the Christian life. He serves as the General Editor of the ESV Bible and as the Theological Editor for the *ESV Study Bible*.

LANE T. DENNIS is President of Crossway, a not-for-profit publishing ministry. Dr. Dennis earned his PhD from Northwestern University. He is Chair of the ESV Bible Translation Oversight Committee and Executive Editor of the *ESV Study Bible*.

DANE C. ORTLUND is Executive Vice President of Bible Publishing and Bible Publisher at Crossway. He is a graduate of Covenant Theological Seminary (MDiv, ThM) and Wheaton College (BA, PhD). Dr. Ortlund has authored several books and scholarly articles in the areas of Bible, theology, and Christian living.

HAGGAI, ZECHARIAH, AND MALACHI

A 12-WEEK STUDY

Stephen M. Coleman

CROSSWAY®

WHEATON, ILLINOIS

Knowing the Bible: Haggai, Zechariah, and Malachi, A 12-Week Study

Copyright © 2018 by Crossway

Published by Crossway
    1300 Crescent Street
    Wheaton, Illinois 60187

Cover design: Simplicated Studio

First printing 2018

Printed in the United States of America

Trade paperback ISBN: 978-1-4335-5733-0
ePub ISBN: 978-1-4335-5736-1
PDF ISBN: 978-1-4335-5734-7
Mobipocket ISBN: 978-1-4335-5735-4

Crossway is a publishing ministry of Good News Publishers.

VP			27	26	25	24	23	22	21	20	19	18
15	14	13	12	11	10	9	8	7	6	5	4	3	2	1

TABLE OF CONTENTS

▲

SERIES PREFACE

KNOWING THE BIBLE, as the series title indicates, was created to help readers know and understand the meaning, the message, and the God of the Bible. Each volume in the series consists of 12 units that progressively take the reader through a clear, concise study of one or more books of the Bible. In this way, any given volume can fruitfully be used in a 12-week format either in group study, such as in a church-based context, or in individual study. Of course, these 12 studies could be completed in fewer or more than 12 weeks, as convenient, depending on the context in which they are used.

Each study unit gives an overview of the text at hand before digging into it with a series of questions for reflection or discussion. The unit then concludes by highlighting the gospel of grace in each passage ("Gospel Glimpses"), identifying whole-Bible themes that occur in the passage ("Whole-Bible Connections"), and pinpointing Christian doctrines that are affirmed in the passage ("Theological Soundings").

The final component to each unit is a section for reflecting on personal and practical implications from the passage at hand. The layout provides space for recording responses to the questions proposed, and we think readers need to do this to get the full benefit of the exercise. The series also includes definitions of key words. These definitions are indicated by a note number in the text and are found at the end of each chapter.

Lastly, to help understand the Bible in this deeper way, we urge readers to use the ESV Bible and the *ESV Study Bible*, which are available in various print and digital formats, including online editions at esv.org. The *Knowing the Bible* series is also available online.

May the Lord greatly bless your study as you seek to know him through knowing his Word.

J. I. Packer
Lane T. Dennis

WEEK 1: OVERVIEW

Waiting is hard. Waiting in times of hardship, struggle, and temptation is even harder. Known as the postexilic[1] prophets, Haggai, Zechariah, and Malachi minister to God's people in such a time of difficult waiting. The Jews who have returned (or whose ancestors returned) to Jerusalem from Babylon in 538 BC could see in their return the fulfillment of God's gracious promises of deliverance made through the prophets of old (e.g., Deut. 30:1–10; Isa. 52:7–12; Jer. 29:10–14). Their return, however, is only a partial fulfillment, and they quickly discover that the fullness of Israel's glorious restoration still lies in the future.

This period of waiting presents God's people with many challenges. They exist under the domination of the foreign pagan empire of Persia, and their efforts to rebuild a temple and city meet with opposition from neighboring peoples (Ezra 4). They lack a Davidic king on the throne, and the rebuilt temple lacks its former glory (Hag. 2:3). Doubt, discouragement, and despair gain a foothold in the hearts of this postexilic community.

Perhaps the most difficult challenge, however, is the challenge of trusting God's Word when so much of their experience is preaching a different message. When Israel considers the international scene, God's sovereignty is far from evident, and Israel's future glory seems far from certain. Nevertheless, the postexilic prophets pronounce with great boldness the Lord's sovereignty over the nations and his commitment to bless his chosen people. Like that of the prophets before them, the call of the postexilic prophets is first and foremost a call to faith: faith in God, faith in his gracious promises, and faith in the coming Messiah.

Placing the Postexilic Prophets in the Larger Story

In 586 BC, the ultimate covenant curse came upon God's people in the form of national exile. Because Israel persisted in unbelief and violated the terms of the covenant in the most grievous ways imaginable, the Lord brought the Babylonian army in judgment upon his own people (2 Kings 21:10–16). The temple was destroyed, the Davidic king removed from his throne, the royal city razed to the ground, and God's chosen people were exiled from the Promised Land. All hope would have been lost except for God's promise that his grace would triumph over judgment (Deut. 30:1–10; Jer. 29:10–11; 33:14–22), and that through a remnant of his people he would fulfill his covenant promises to bless the nations through the seed of Abraham (Gen. 12:3; Isa. 10:20–23).

Almost 50 years later, in 538 BC, Cyrus the Great, king of Persia, released the Jews from captivity. He commissioned them to rebuild the temple to their God and reinstitute worship according to their laws (Ezra 1). Although the initial building project began with great energy and optimism, external pressures as well as internal struggle caused the building project to grind to a halt. Eighteen years later, in 520 BC, the temple remained in ruins as the people of God had become preoccupied with securing their own worldly comforts. Into this situation the postexilic prophets come with a powerful word of both warning and promise. They warn Israel of the dangers of forsaking their God and remind Israel of God's unwavering commitment to his people's welfare. These three themes come to dominate the message of the postexilic prophets: God's sovereignty over the nations, his presence with his people, and his commitment to the future glory of both Israel and the nations. With these truths pressed firmly on their hearts, Israel will have to wait with patience for the final and ultimate fulfillment of God's promises, when their deliverance will be complete and the God of Israel will be recognized as sovereign over the whole world.

Key Verse

"Rejoice greatly, O daughter of Zion! Shout aloud, O daughter of Jerusalem! Behold, your king is coming to you; righteous and having salvation is he, humble and mounted on a donkey, on a colt, the foal of a donkey." (Zech. 9:9)

Date and Historical Background

Determining the date of Haggai and much of Zechariah is refreshingly straightforward. The oracles[2] in Haggai and in Zechariah 1–8 are dated with reference to the reigning Persian emperor, Darius I. Most are delivered in his second regnal year, 520–519 BC (Hag. 1:1; 2:1, 10, 20; Zech. 1:1, 7), and one in his fourth, 518 BC (Zech. 7:1). In many cases, the date of the oracle contributes to the message itself. For example, Haggai announces Israel's future glory during the Feast of Tabernacles, an apt occasion for pointing God's people toward the future (Hag. 2:1). Zechariah 9–14 is more difficult to date, as the prophecies seem to address circumstances very different from those addressed in chapters 1–8. The most likely explanation is that these oracles come from a later period in the prophet's ministry, a time when the initial optimism and obedience surrounding the rebuilding of the temple have given way to corruption in the leadership and a return to idolatry (Zech. 10:1–3).

Not much is known about the personal life of the prophet Haggai. The focus of the book bearing his name is not so much on the prophet himself but on the message that he brings. We know only slightly more about Zechariah. He is identified as the "son of Berechiah, son of Iddo" (Zech. 1:1), making him a member of a priestly family who returned from Babylon (see Neh. 12:4). In all likelihood, Zechariah himself is a priest, and his prophecies exhibit a clear interest in the temple and priesthood (Zechariah 3; 4:1–4; 6:9–14).

In contrast to Haggai and Zechariah, the date of Malachi is a bit more difficult to determine with certainty. Little is known about the prophet Malachi, including when he lives and ministers. That he serves during the postexilic period is clear from the mention of a governor rather than a king (Mal. 1:8). Furthermore, the fact that his prophetic "lawsuit" is directed at the priests suggests that at least a good portion of his ministry takes place in or around Jerusalem sometime after the rebuilding of the temple. Like its date, the historical background of Malachi is similarly blurry. It is perhaps significant that the issues Malachi addresses resemble those addressed by the postexilic leaders Ezra and Nehemiah (e.g., a corrupt priesthood, see Mal. 1:6–2:9 and Neh. 13:4–9; and marriage to foreign wives, see Mal. 2:11–12; Ezra 9–10; Neh. 13:1–3). Thus a mid-fifth-century date for Malachi seems most likely.

As You Get Started

What is your current understanding of what life is like for postexilic Israel? What challenges do they face, and what resources do they have to meet these challenges?

Are there any aspects of the prophets in general, or these postexilic prophets in particular, that you find particularly confusing or difficult to understand?

The historical background of Haggai and Zechariah is recorded for us in the book of Ezra. Take some time to read Ezra 1–6 and write down observations about key figures of the period as well as the circumstances surrounding the rebuilding of the temple.

Outline

Haggai

  I. Introduction: Reluctant Rebuilders (1:1–2)

   A. Characters (1:1)

   B. Context (1:2)

  II. Consider Your Ways: Fruitless Prosperity (1:3–12)

   A. Work without satisfaction (1:3–11)

   B. General response: obedience and fear (1:12)

  III. Promise and Progress (1:13–15a)

   A. God's promise (1:13)

   B. Specific response: work begins (1:14–15a)

  IV. The Former and Latter Glory of This House (1:15b–2:9)

   A. Comparing past and present (1:15b–2:3)

   B. Acting based on the past (2:4–5)

   C. An image of God's house restored (2:6–9)

B. The second oracle: the people and their leaders (12:1–14:21)

1. The restoration and renewal of God's people (12:1–13:6)
    a. Jerusalem's triumph and the nations' doom (12:1–9)
    b. Mourning for sin (12:10–14)
    c. Cleansing from sin and idolatry (13:1–6)
2. Judgment and transformation (13:7–14:21)
    a. The shepherd struck and the flock scattered (13:7–9)
    b. Jerusalem's judgment, deliverance, and exaltation (14:1–11)
    c. The nations humbled and brought into submission (14:12–21)

Malachi

Heading (1:1)

A. *First Disputation*: Does God make a distinction between the good and the arrogantly wicked? God's elective love vindicated in his judgment (1:2–5)
B. *Second Disputation*: Israel's begrudging offerings condemned (1:6–2:9)
C. *Third Disputation*: Marriage to an idolater—and divorce based on aversion—condemned by the Lord, who is witness to the covenant of marriage (2:10–16)
C'. *Fourth Disputation*: The Lord is a witness against adultery and other moral offenses (2:17–3:5)
B'. *Fifth Disputation*: Israel's begrudging offerings condemned (3:6–12)
A'. *Sixth Disputation*: Does God make a distinction between the good and the arrogantly wicked? God's elective love vindicated in his judgment (3:13–4:3)

Conclusion (4:4–6)

> ### ▶ As You Finish This Unit . . .

Take a few minutes to ask God to grant you ears to hear and eyes to see the wonders of the gospel of Christ promised and foretold by these prophets.

Definitions

[1] **Exile** – Several relocations of large groups of Israelites/Jews have occurred throughout history, but "the exile" typically refers to the Babylonian exile, that is, Nebuchadnezzar's relocation of residents of the southern kingdom of Judah to Babylon in 586 BC (residents of the northern kingdom of Israel had been resettled by Assyria in 722 BC). After Babylon came under Persian rule, several waves of Jewish exiles returned and repopulated Judah.

[2] **Oracle** – From Latin "to speak." In the Bible, refers to a divine pronouncement delivered through a human agent.

WEEK 2: THE TIME IS NOW

Haggai 1:1–15a

▲

The Place of the Passage

In the year 538 BC, a remnant of God's people returned from Babylon to the Promised Land with the intention of rebuilding the temple and reinstituting worship of Yahweh[1] in Jerusalem. Yet, 18 years later, the temple still lies in ruins, the people are barely surviving on meager crops and insufficient water, and a general discouragement has set in among the postexilic community in Jerusalem. Into this context of discouragement and spiritual disorientation, the word of the Lord comes to his people through his prophet Haggai, transforming Jerusalem. In this opening oracle Haggai offers a powerful challenge to the spiritual lethargy of God's people, identifying the secret idols of their hearts and calling them to renewed faith and obedience.

The Big Picture

God confronts his people's idolatries and misplaced priorities, calling them to renewed faith, repentance, and the fruit of that repentance—exhibited in their faithfulness in rebuilding the temple.

> ## Reflection and Discussion

Read through the complete passage for this study, Haggai 1:1–15a. Then review the questions below and write your notes on them. (For further background, see the *ESV Study Bible*, pages 1744–1745; available online at www.esvbible.org.)

1. Haggai's Historical Setting (1:1)

The opening date formula (Hag. 1:1) places Haggai's prophecy on August 29, 520 BC, three months after the grain and corn harvest (June–July) and toward the end of the fruit tree harvest. In the Jewish calendar, the first day of the month was a holy day and a festival to the Lord. The Jews would therefore have time to consider the quantity and quality of their harvest thus far and would be looking forward, no doubt with a great deal of apprehension, to what the rest of the harvest would bring. What is the importance of this setting for the message that follows?

Although it has implications for the entire postexilic community, Haggai's message is spoken directly to Zerubbabel, the governor, and Joshua, the high priest. How do these two individuals represent the two great institutions that were to govern Israel's faith and life? Why is it significant that the command to rebuild the temple should be directed toward the governor and the high priest?

2. The Lord Has a Complaint (1:2–11)

In verse 2, the Lord issues his indictment: "These people say the time has not yet come to rebuild the house of the LORD." Although reasons are not given for why the people believe "the time has not yet come," we can imagine a number of excuses they might make. From what you know about the conditions of postexilic Jerusalem, what might they point to as justification for delaying the rebuilding of the temple? How do we make similar excuses for neglecting God's calling on our own lives?

How do the people's lives belie their excuses? What is the real cause of Israel's delay?

In verse 6, God describes the frustrations Israel has experienced because of its sin: "You have sown much, and harvested little. You eat, but you never have enough; you drink, but you never have your fill. You clothe yourselves, but no one is warm. And he who earns wages does so to put them into a bag with holes." What insight does this give us into the nature of idolatry?

15

In verses 9–10, God announces that the suffering Israel is experiencing is ultimately from his hand. For what purpose does God bring such hardship upon his people (compare Heb. 12:7–11)?

Between the two announcements of covenant curses (Hag. 1:6 and vv. 9–11) comes the heart of the prophet's message: "Go up to the hills and bring wood and build the house, that I may take pleasure in it and that I may be glorified, says the LORD" (v. 8). How will the temple bring glory to God?

3. The People's (Surprising) Response (1:12–15a)

In verse 12 we read of Israel's response to the prophetic word. From what you know of Israel's history, how is their response both surprising and encouraging?

Israel's response is a wonderful picture of true repentance. What elements of repentance do you see in the people's response to the word of God?

God expresses his presence with his people in those wonderful words, "I am with you, declares the LORD" (v. 13). Notice that the Lord's presence is not the *result* of Israel's obedience in building the temple but the *basis* and *motivation* for their obedience in doing so. How does this dynamic reflect the motivation for our own obedience today?

Zerubbabel, Joshua, and all the people respond to the prophet's summons by working faithfully and diligently to rebuild the house of the Lord (v. 12). According to verses 14–15, what is the ultimate source of their faithfulness and success? What does this teach us about God's work in our lives?

Read through the following three sections on *Gospel Glimpses*, *Whole-Bible Connections*, and *Theological Soundings*. Then take time to consider the *Personal Implications* these sections may have for you.

Gospel Glimpses

REPENTANCE. The account of Israel's response to the word of God through his prophet (Hag. 1:12–15) is a remarkable picture of heartfelt repentance. We are told that the people "obeyed the voice of the LORD" and "feared the LORD" (v. 12). The "fear of the LORD" in the Old Testament is roughly equivalent to what the New Testament means by faith: receiving and resting upon the promises of God. Implicit in Israel's actions is the acknowledgment of their sinful behavior, and explicitly mentioned is their obedience, which is the fruit of faith and true repentance.

17

GOD WITH US. The announcement that God is with his people is central to Haggai's message. Adam and Eve lost God's presence in the garden through their single act of rebellion. Yet no sooner had they lost it through human sin than God promised to renew and reestablish his communion with his image-bearers through his own sovereign and gracious initiative (Gen. 3:15). This promise, summarized memorably in the name Immanuel, "God with us" (Isa. 7:14), was for the postexilic community (and the exiles before them) truly good news. That "God is with us" meant that while Israel's sin had led to their exile, it could not sever the bond of God's covenant love for his people.

Whole-Bible Connections

THE TRUE TEMPLE. The temple, like the tabernacle before it, was a symbol of God's gracious presence with his people. Both the tabernacle erected in the wilderness and the temple built by King Solomon serve as watershed moments in redemptive history in which God is dramatically displayed as present with his people. Yet these physical structures were merely symbols of the true temple, Jesus Christ, who would "tabernacle among us" (see John 1:14) and who would declare to his disciples, "Destroy this temple, and in three days I will raise it up" (John 2:19). Jesus is the fullness of God's presence. God desired a temple not because he needs a house in which to live (see 2 Sam. 7:7) but because he created and redeemed his people so that they might worship him in Spirit and truth. The temple displayed that God has made a way for sinful men and women to dwell in the presence of a holy God through the blood of a sacrifice and the ministry of a high priest.

Theological Soundings

IDOLATRY. The prophet's denunciation of the people's misplaced priorities reveals something about the nature of idolatry: the idols of our heart make promises they cannot keep. They promise that if we serve, for example, comfort, wealth, power, or pleasure, we will experience deep satisfaction and peace. The reality is that serving anything other than the one true God leads ultimately to only dissatisfaction and emptiness (Eccles. 2:1–11). Throughout the Bible, God's people are called to recognize the false promises of idols for what they are: lies that lead away from the true peace that comes only from knowing and worshiping the living God.

GOD'S SOVEREIGNTY AND MAN'S RESPONSIBILITY. Although it is in many respects a mystery, the Bible unapologetically affirms the twin truths that God has decreed and is sovereign over all that comes to pass, and yet that mankind bears moral responsibility for his actions. We see both realities at work in Haggai 1:1–15a. In verse 12, we are told that the leaders and all the people "obeyed the voice of the LORD their God, and the words of Haggai the prophet." Yet as the passage comes to a close, we are told that the ultimate origin of the people's obedience is God himself: "The LORD stirred up the spirit of Zerubbabel the son of Shealtiel, governor of Judah, and the spirit of Joshua the son of Jehozadak, the high priest, and the spirit of all the remnant of the people" (v. 14) The apostle Paul similarly holds these twin truths in tension when he commands the Philippian Christians, "Work out your own salvation with fear and trembling, for it is God who works in you, both to will and to work for his good pleasure" (Phil. 2:12b–13).

Personal Implications

Take time to reflect on the implications of Haggai 1:1–15a for your own life today. Consider what you have learned that might lead you to praise God, repent of sin, and trust in his gracious promises. Write down your reflections under the three headings we have considered and on the passage as a whole.

1. Gospel Glimpses

2. Whole-Bible Connections

3. Theological Soundings

4. Haggai 1:1–15a

_____

_____

_____

_____

_____

_____

▶ As You Finish This Unit . . .

Take a moment now to ask God for the grace of repentance so that through the illuminating work of the Holy Spirit you might acknowledge the sinful affections of your heart and flee to Jesus Christ, the true temple, by faith.

Definition

[1] **Yahweh** – The likely English form of the name represented by the Hebrew letters YHWH. The Lord revealed this unique name for himself (meaning "I am") to Moses at the burning bush, telling him to instruct the Israelites to call on him by this name (Ex. 3:14–15). English translations of the Bible usually render this term as "Lord," with small capital letters. (YHWH can also be translated "God," in small capitals.)

WEEK 3: GOD'S PROMISE OF A GLORIOUS FUTURE

Haggai 1:15b–2:23

The Place of the Passage

The two great pillars of Israel's faith were the temple and the kingship (see Ps. 78:67–72). Both, however, had been destroyed at the time of the exile (Jer. 52:1–16). In the concluding oracles of Haggai, we see both institutions being resurrected in a sense, though only as dim reflections of their former selves. Although lacking its glory of old, the temple is being rebuilt. Although ruling as a governor in the employ of the Persian Empire, a descendant of David is nevertheless leading God's people in the person of Zerubbabel. Things are far from ideal for the postexilic community; nevertheless, the temple and the governor serve Israel as reminders, foreshadows, or types[1] of the true temple and perfect Davidic king who would come in the person of Jesus.

The Big Picture

God assures his discouraged people that through the temple and the king he will establish Israel's eternal blessedness.

> **Reflection and Discussion**

Read through the complete passage for this study, Haggai 1:15b–2:23. Then review the questions below and write your notes on them. (For further background, see the *ESV Study Bible*, pages 1745–1747; available online at www.esvbible.org.)

1. Work, for God Is with You (1:15b–2:9)

The second oracle is dated to the twenty-first day of the seventh month of the second year of Darius (Hag. 1:15b–2:1), placing it at the end of the annual Feast of Booths (Lev. 23:33–43). What event did the Feast of Booths commemorate, and how does knowledge of this timing shed light on these verses?

The second temple was approximately the same size as the first and furnished in much the same way. In what sense, then, does the second temple lack its former glory (compare Ex. 40:34; 1 Kings 8:10–11)? What is God's purpose for his people in giving them a less than glorious temple?

What two promises does God give the postexilic community to strengthen them in the difficult task of rebuilding the temple (Hag. 2:4–9)?

In verses 6–9, the prophet announces an imminent cosmic upheaval. While this may seem like a terrifying prospect at first, the result is actually a message of hope for God's people. What is the result of God's "shaking" of the nations? How does this upheaval set the world in its proper order?

2. God's Promise to Bless a Defiled People (2:10–19)

In Haggai 2:10–13, the prophet approaches the priests with a case study regarding the contaminating properties of clean and unclean objects. How would you summarize the principles of contamination as outlined by the priests (vv. 12–13)? Which is more powerful, cleanness or uncleanness?

While ritual purity is not necessarily a matter of sin, purity laws are meant to teach Israel something about the nature of sin. What do we learn from Haggai's case study about the power and contaminating properties of sin?

Prior to rebuilding the temple, what problems did Israel experience on account of their ritual impurity (2:14–17)? How does the temple rectify this predicament (vv. 18–19)?

3. The Triumph of the Davidic King (2:20–23)

To describe a future judgment of the world, Haggai uses language that draws heavily on God's earlier acts of redemption (vv. 21–22). The word "overthrow" alludes to God's judgment against Sodom and Gomorrah (Gen. 19:25). "Destroy" recalls God's action in rooting out the Canaanites from the land before Joshua (Deut. 7:23–24; 31:3–4). Horses and riders "going down" evokes the memory of God's triumph over the Egyptian army at the Red Sea (Ex. 15:4–5). Why does God describe Israel's future in terms that recall her past?

Zerubbabel is given the designation "my servant" (Hag. 2:23), a title used often for God's agents of deliverance, especially the Davidic king (Josh. 1:2; 2 Sam. 3:18; Ps. 89:3). How is this an appropriate designation for Zerubbabel? In what way does Zerubbabel's faithfulness to God foreshadow Jesus' work of temple building (see 1 Pet. 2:4–5)?

God says that he will make Zerubbabel "like a signet ring." How does this reverse God's previous actions toward the Davidic kingship (Jer. 22:24–25)? How is this in keeping with the character of the Davidic covenant (2 Sam. 7:12–16)?

Read through the following three sections on *Gospel Glimpses, Whole-Bible Connections*, and *Theological Soundings*. Then take time to consider the *Personal Implications* these sections may have for you.

Gospel Glimpses

FEAST OF BOOTHS. Even after Israel had entered the Promised Land, they were commanded to celebrate the Feast of Booths annually (Lev. 23:33–43). This celebration served to point Israel to the past, reminding them of God's provision in the wilderness. However, it also pointed Israel toward the future, reminding them that the land of Canaan was not their ultimate home but only a type of their heavenly home (compare Heb. 11:14). The Feast of Booths is the perfect time for the word of the Lord to come to the postexilic community, reminding them of the glorious future he has in store for them.

PURIFIED WORSHIP. "What they offer there is unclean" (Hag. 2:14b). When Israel lacked a temple, even their best offerings were unacceptable to God because they were contaminated by the unclean hands that offered them. Yet when Israel approaches God in the temple, through the mediation of priests and the blood of sacrifices, even Israel's imperfect worship becomes acceptable and pleasing to God when offered in faith. The temple is a picture of Christ: when Christians approach God in worship through faith in Christ, they too hear the words of gospel promise, "From this day on I will bless you" (Hag. 2:19; compare Heb. 4:14–16).

Whole-Bible Connections

DAVIDIC KINGSHIP RESTORED. Although in Jeremiah's day God had torn off and discarded the Davidic King Jehoiachin as a king might discard a precious signet ring (Jer. 22:24–25), in Haggai's day he renews his commitment to the line of David in his promise to Zerubbabel (Hag. 2:23). In contrast to his treatment of King Saul, God had promised David that although he would discipline his descendants with the rod of men, his steadfast love would not depart from them (2 Sam. 7:14–15). Jesus came in the line of David and was recognized by many to be the messianic Son of David (Matt. 1:1–6; Mark 10:47). In Jesus, we meet the true King of Israel, one who would build God's house in his own body and subsequently in his people.

PURIFICATION. Israel's purity laws pertain to external realities (e.g., diet, physical health, contact with the dead), yet are meant to teach Israel, among other things, about the holiness of God, the nature of sin, and the need for atonement.

In Jesus' ministry, we see something of the reversal of the principles of contamination. Typically, touching a leper, a woman with a discharge, or a corpse would make someone unclean and would leave the leper, woman, or corpse in a state of ritual impurity. However, when Jesus touches these individuals, they are healed, purified, and, through faith, forgiven (Mark 1:40–45; 5:21–43). Jesus is able to do so because of his power over sin and death and because of his willingness to switch places with these individuals (and with us) by becoming unclean and defiled on the cross (2 Cor. 5:21).

Theological Soundings

COVENANT. God deals with his creation by means of covenants, that is, formal relationships often established by oath and attended with sanctions. The Bible contains many divine-human covenants that serve as the basis for God's actions toward his creation. After the fall of mankind into sin, God's covenantal relationships with his people take on a fundamentally gracious character. In Haggai 1:15b–2:23 we see two different covenants undergirding God's relationship with the postexilic community. The "covenant that I made with you when you came out of Egypt" (v. 5) refers to the Mosaic, or Sinaitic, covenant. Israel is once again a theocratic nation, governed by laws delivered by Moses at Mount Sinai. This covenant will persist until it is fulfilled by the work of Christ (see Heb. 8:8–13). The Davidic covenant is in view in God's promise to Zerubbabel (Hag. 2:23). Because God's promises to David were ultimately unconditional, the sinfulness of Israel's kings could not derail God's commitment to establish a son of David on his throne forever.

Personal Implications

Take time to reflect on the implications of Haggai 1:15b–2:23 for your own life today. Consider what you have learned that might lead you to praise God, repent of sin, and trust in his gracious promises. Write down your reflections under the three headings we have considered and on the passage as a whole.

1. Gospel Glimpses

2. Whole-Bible Connections

3. Theological Soundings

4. Haggai 1:15b–2:23

As You Finish This Unit . . .

Take a moment now to consider the privilege it is to see the fulfillment of God's promises of a true temple and faithful king in the person and work of Jesus Christ.

Definition

[1] **Typology** – A method of interpretation in which a real, historical object, place, or person is recognized as a pattern or foreshadowing (a "type") of some later object, place, or person. For example, the Bible presents Adam as a "type" of Christ (Rom. 5:14).

WEEK 4: GLORY IN HER MIDST

Zechariah 1:1–2:13

▲

After delivering an introductory oracle warning the postexilic community against repeating the sins of their forefathers (Zech. 1:1–6), the prophet Zechariah receives a series of eight night visions (1:7–6:8). These visions are God's answer to the obstacles the Jews have faced in rebuilding the temple, such as discouragement, oppression, spiritual lethargy, and doubt about the Lord's commitment to his people. The visions have a dreamlike quality, featuring fantastic and bizarre figures, images, and scenes characteristic of apocalyptic[1] literature. They serve as a window into the spiritual forces at work behind the mundane realities of the physical world. Although sometimes the details of the visions are obscure, the overall message is clear: God will triumph over the evil forces of this world and lead his people into a glorious future.

The Big Picture

God responds to the sufferings of his people by announcing that very soon he will overthrow their oppressors and establish his eternal, universal kingdom in righteousness.

Reflection and Discussion

Read through the complete passage for this study, Zechariah 1:1–2:13. Then review the questions below and write your notes on them. (For further background, see the *ESV Study Bible*, pages 1753–1755; available online at www.esvbible.org.)

1. Call to Repentance (1:1–6)

In Zechariah 1:1–6, the prophet summarizes Israel's history leading up to the exile. How does he characterize that period of Israel's history? What lesson does he want the postexilic community to learn from God's dealings with their forefathers?

The opening oracle contains a strong word of warning and a promise of judgment. However, there is another message here as well. Where do we find a message of mercy and grace in these verses?

"Your fathers, where are they? And the prophets, do they live forever? But my words and my statutes, which I commanded my servants the prophets, did they not overtake your fathers?" (vv. 5–6a). What do these questions teach us about the character of God's Word? Why is it important for the postexilic community to be reminded of this?

29

2. Vision 1: The Lord's Horsemen (1:7–17)

The Persian Empire was known for its skilled horsemanship. Persia used horses in battle and to maintain their elaborate network of communications by which the emperor could keep watch on even the farthest reaches of his vast empire. In the first night vision, Zechariah sees that the Persian emperor is not the only one whose spies range throughout the world. The Lord has sent out his own horsemen to spy and to report (1:10). What does this teach us about God's knowledge? How would this be an encouragement to the postexilic community?

Typically, we would think that the angels' message that "all the earth remains at rest" (v. 11) would be good news. However, the angel of the Lord responds with a loud cry of lamentation (v. 12). Why does the news that the nations are at rest evoke such a strong lament from the angel of the Lord?

In verses 15–17, the Lord responds to the spies' report and the angel's lament. How would you describe God's posture toward Israel and the nations? How does this revelation address one of the pressing concerns of the postexilic community?

----

3. Vision 2: Judah's Oppressors Cast Down (1:18–21)

Throughout Scripture, a horn serves as a symbol for military strength and power (e.g., Deut. 33:17; Ps. 75:4; Dan. 7:19–22). In Zechariah 1:18, the prophet sees four horns. The type of horn is uncertain; some have suggested that Zechariah sees the horns of a helmet, an altar, or an animal. What (or whom) do these horns represent? How does their fate fulfill the Abrahamic promise (see Gen. 12:3)?

Following the horns are the four craftsmen. They have come to "terrify" and to "cast down the horns of the nations" who scattered Judah (Zech. 1:21). What does the vision of the four craftsmen reveal about God's sovereignty over the nations? How does their punishment reflect their offense?

4: Vision 3: A City without Walls (2:1–13)

The third night vision (2:1–13) is essentially the flip side of the second vision. Not only will God reverse the fortunes of Israel's enemies who are at rest in their rebellion and pride (1:18–21); he will also reverse the fortunes of his own people and prosper them beyond anything they could ask or imagine. According to Zechariah 2:1–4, in what ways does God promise to bless Israel in the future?

Living in an unwalled city would be deeply unsettling for Israel, leaving them insecure, vulnerable, and defenseless. However, the message that Jerusalem will be inhabited as "villages without walls" is clearly good news for the people of God (2:4). Why would this be the case?

How is the announcement that God will be a "wall of fire all around" Jerusalem and "the glory in her midst" (2:5) a fulfillment of God's gracious promises throughout the Old Testament (compare Lev. 26:11–12; 1 Kings 8:10–11; Ezek. 37:27–28)?

In Zechariah 2:6–13, the Lord gives commands to three different groups of people: those who dwell in Babylon (vv. 6–9), the daughter of Zion (i.e., those who have returned to Jerusalem; v. 10), and "all flesh" (i.e., the nations). What is God's unique message to each group, and what is his ultimate goal for them?

Read through the following three sections on *Gospel Glimpses*, *Whole-Bible Connections*, and *Theological Soundings*. Then take time to consider the *Personal Implications* these sections may have for you.

Gospel Glimpses

GOD'S BLESSING EXTENDS TO THE NATIONS. God's commitment to bless Abraham and his offspring has always had a universal scope. In Genesis 12:3 God says to Abram, "I will bless those who bless you, and him who dishonors you I will curse." As God renews his commitment to bless the postexilic Jewish community living in and around Jerusalem, he also reminds them of his posture toward the nations. Just as his judgment against them in the exile was not his final word for the Jews, so also his word of judgment against the nations (Zech. 1:15) is not his final word for them, either. In Zechariah 2:11 God promises, "Many nations shall join themselves to the LORD in that day, and shall be my people." The Gentiles who in Zechariah's day were "not my people" will in Jesus' day become "my people" (Rom. 9:24–25; 1 Pet. 2:10).

GOD RETURNS. In Ezekiel 10, the prophet witnessed God's departure from his temple. The reason is clear: Israel's sin so defiled the holy place that it had become an unfit habitation for a holy God (Ezek. 9:9–10). In Zechariah 1–2, the prophet announces the Lord's return to his temple. In this return, Israel sees that her sin cannot separate her from the steadfast, covenantal love of God, and that his grace for his elect will ultimately triumph over his judgment. Although the Lord returned his temple in Zechariah's day (1:16), there was yet to come a fuller and greater manifestation of God's glory returning to his temple. Israel would have to continue to wait until the coming of Christ for God truly to dwell with his people (John 1:14), which itself would be only a foretaste of his eternal dwelling with them (Rev. 21:3).

Whole-Bible Connections

THE ANGEL OF THE LORD. Although the Lord has countless angels, throughout Scripture one angel stands out as unique. This angel is designated "the angel of the LORD." He is clearly a heavenly messenger, but at times he also exhibits divine qualities. For instance, this angel makes the ground around him holy (Josh. 5:13–15), and at other times he speaks as God himself (Gen. 22:11–18; Ex. 3:2–6). This has led many theologians to suggest that this angel is an appearance of the preincarnate Son, one who speaks at times to God, at other times for God, and yet at other times *as* God. Here we seem to gain a small glimpse into the mystery and wonder of the Trinity in the Old Testament.

Theological Soundings

THE RELIABILITY OF GOD'S WORD. Ever since Adam and Eve succumbed to the serpent's question, "Did God actually say . . . ?" (Gen. 3:1), the perennial temptation of God's people has been to doubt the truthfulness, goodness, and reliability of his Word. Sinful hearts doubt their Creator, finding it easier to rely on what they think, feel, or experience instead of on the Word of God. Yet, without apology, God's Word declares itself to be true and reliable in every way (Psalm 119), and God's people are called to hold it as their ultimate authority in all matters pertaining to faith and life (2 Tim. 3:16–17). In this way, Christians reflect their Savior, who responded to the Devil's temptation by stating, "It is written, 'Man shall not live by bread alone, but by every word that comes from the mouth of God'" (Matt. 4:4; compare Deut. 8:3).

OMNISCIENCE. The Bible clearly teaches that God is all-knowing (Ps. 139:1–6; Matt. 10:30). Not only does he know everything that has taken place in the past; he knows all that is happening in the present and all that will happen in the future (Isa. 42:9), for past, present, and future are all one eternal present to the One who stands outside of time and space. This doctrine has many practical implications. For example, God's omniscience is a sobering warning to those who think that their evil deeds will go unpunished (Ps. 1:5–6). This doctrine also serves as a comforting reminder that God knows and cares about the suffering of his people and will one day act to vindicate both himself as the God of justice and his people as those who belong to him (Zech. 12:7–9).

Personal Implications

Take time to reflect on the implications of Zechariah 1:1–2:13 for your own life today. Consider what you have learned that might lead you to praise God, repent of sin, and trust in his gracious promises. Write down your reflections under the three headings we have considered and on the passage as a whole.

1. Gospel Glimpses

2. Whole-Bible Connections

3. Theological Soundings

_____

_____

_____

_____

_____

_____

4. Zechariah 1:1–2:13

_____

_____

_____

_____

_____

▶ As You Finish This Unit . . .

Take a moment now to thank God for his wonderful promise that the wickedness, oppression, and sin of this present evil age is not the end of the story; and that his victory over evil, which has begun in the resurrection Christ, will one day be manifest throughout the whole world.

Definition

[1] **Apocalyptic** – The distinctive literary form of the book of Revelation and of chapters 7–12 of Daniel. These parts of Scripture include revelation about the future, highly symbolic imagery, and the underlying belief that God himself will one day end the world in its present form and establish his kingdom on earth.

WEEK 5: A PURIFIED PRIEST AND A FAITHFUL KING

Zechariah 3:1–4:14

The Place of the Passage

Of the eight night visions (Zech. 1:7–6:8), visions four and five (chs. 3–4) form the centerpiece of these fantastic revelations both structurally, in that they come in the middle of the series, and theologically, in that they provide the basis for God's redemptive work depicted in the surrounding visions. These two visions feature the two central figures of the early postexilic period: Joshua the high priest; and Zerubbabel, the scion of David and governor of the postexilic community. God called these men to lead Israel in rebuilding the temple, and through their faithfulness this symbol of God's presence and favor would once again stand in the midst of his people (Hag. 1:1). In the two central night visions, then, the prophet Zechariah is given a deeper understanding of the work of the Messiah as the Great High Priest and King of his people.

The Big Picture

Through the work of a pure Priest and the obedience of a faithful King, God will purify his people from their sins and establish his permanent presence in their midst.

> ## Reflection and Discussion

Read through the complete passage for this study, Zechariah 3:1–4:14. Then review the questions below and write your notes on them. (For further background, see the *ESV Study Bible*, pages 1755–1757; available online at www.esvbible.org.)

1. The High Priest Purified (3:1–10)

The third night vision opens with a courtroom scene. Joshua the high priest stands as the accused, Satan[1] stands as the prosecutor, and the angel of the Lord (a manifestation of God himself) sits in judgment (v. 1). The courtroom drama begins in verse 2. Describe the dramatic action that ensues.

The Lord refers to Joshua as a "brand plucked from the fire" (v. 2). To what does this refer?

In verse 3 it is revealed that Joshua stands in "filthy [literally "excrement covered"] garments." Such attire renders Joshua ritually impure. How does this impure status present a crisis not only for Joshua but also for the entire covenant community?

The Lord not only dismisses the charge against Joshua (v. 2); he also addresses the basis for Satan's accusations. He commands his angels to remove Joshua's filthy garments and to clothe him with pure vestments and a clean turban (vv. 4–5). What spiritual realities are depicted in the actions of undressing and dressing the high priest?

According to Zechariah 3:7–8, what great work will God accomplish through the priest and the king? How does this look back to the Day of Atonement (Lev. 16:21–22, 30–33) and forward to the work of Christ?

The expression "every . . . under his vine and fig tree" is used elsewhere to refer to the prosperity Israel will enjoy under the rule of a faithful king (e.g., 1 Kings 4:25; Mic. 4:4). What does this promise teach us about the failures of Israel's kings? What does this reveal about Christ's victory in the future?

2. The Message of the Lampstand (4:1–5, 10b–14)

While a golden lampstand (or *menorah*) would be reminiscent of the traditional temple furnishing, this lampstand would seem highly unusual to Zechariah.

What is distinctive about the lampstand the prophet sees in his vision (compare Ex. 25:31–40; 2 Chron. 4:7, 20)?

The discussion about the lampstand is interrupted by a message for Zerubbabel (4:6–10a). However, the angel draws our attention back to the lampstand in verses 10b–14. The seven lamps on the bowl are said to be "the eyes of the LORD" (v. 10b). What is their function, and what does this teach us about God? How would this encourage the postexilic community?

The *identity* of the two "anointed ones" (or "sons of new oil"; see ESV footnote) is uncertain. Perhaps they represent Haggai and Zechariah, Joshua and Zerubbabel, or simply two angelic servants. Their *function* is more certain, as they are depicted as two branches connecting the two olive trees to the lampstand. What function do the branches have for the lampstand? What does this symbolize for the covenant community?

3. The Faithful King Builds God's Temple (4:6–10a)

Rebuilding the temple of the Lord in Jerusalem could seem like an impossible task for Zerubbabel, the governor of Judea. How does God encourage and strengthen Zerubbabel for this calling (4:6–7)?

Evidently, God's word to Zerubbabel is a response to those who "despised the day of small things" (v. 10). Some in Zerubbabel's day see the work God is doing in Jerusalem as inconsequential, of little significance in the broad scope of world history (v. 10). What sign does the Lord offer as evidence that he is at work and will fulfill all that he has promised (compare Deut. 18:22)? How might we regard God's means of working in the world as "small things," and what message does Zechariah's vision have for us?

Read through the following three sections on *Gospel Glimpses, Whole-Bible Connections,* and *Theological Soundings.* Then take time to consider the *Personal Implications* these sections may have for you.

Gospel Glimpses

GOD REMOVES INIQUITY. The Bible clearly teaches that because of Adam's sin as well as our own, we all stand like Joshua, defiled and unfit to dwell in the presence of a holy God (Rom. 3:9–18, 23; 5:12–21). Yet the gospel declares that God removes our iniquity through the work of Christ (1 Cor. 6:11). Strikingly, Joshua is completely passive in the entire scene. He does not prepare himself for cleansing. He does not scrub out what he can and leave the difficult stains for God. Joshua's cleansing is a work of God from first to last, and it is received by Joshua as a free gift. Ultimately, such a cleansing is accomplished not by the blood of bulls and goats but only through the shedding of the precious blood of Jesus, the Son of God (Heb. 10:4).

FAITHFUL KING. It is easy to misunderstand God's words to Zerubbabel (Zech. 4:6–7) as being a general promise to all believers that God will overcome any and every obstacle they face in this life. However, Zerubbabel serves Israel as a type of Christ, a foreshadow of the faithful king who will obey God perfectly. Zerubbabel's work of beginning and finishing God's temple anticipates the greater work of Christ, who will build God's spiritual house, constructed of living stones (1 Pet. 2:4–5), of which he is the chief cornerstone (Eph. 2:19–22). Like Zerubbabel, Christ's work seems of little account during his earthly ministry; but, also like Zerubbabel, God rewards Christ's faithfulness. In his resurrection, Jesus begins building his church in such a way that the gates of hell itself cannot prevail against it (Matt. 16:18).

Whole-Bible Connections

THE DAY OF SMALL THINGS. The constant challenge for God's people of every age is to evaluate reality according to God's standards rather than the world's. While looking for the next king of Israel, even godly Samuel had to be reminded that "man looks on the outward appearance, but the LORD looks on the heart" (1 Sam. 16:7). Naaman the Syrian almost walked away from God's healing grace because he considered the Jordan River to be insufficient for the task of healing him (2 Kings 5:1–14). In Zechariah's day, many in the postexilic community had a difficult time seeing how their little temple in a backwater town could possibly be used by God to bring salvation to the world. A constant theme throughout Scripture is that God uses the most humble and unexpected means to accomplish his saving purposes. The clearest evidence of this is the cross, where God uses the crucifixion of his Son to ransom a people for himself. Still today, God uses the humble means of his Word and sacraments to bring new life to his elect.

THE BRANCH. Jeremiah once prophesied, "David shall never lack a man to sit on the throne of the house of Israel, and the Levitical priests shall never lack a man in my presence to offer burnt offerings, to burn grain offerings, and to make sacrifices forever" (Jer. 33:17–18). About 70 years after Jeremiah spoke these words, Zechariah sees in Joshua's installation as high priest a sign of the coming Branch, the royal figure in the line of David. This figure would come in the person of Jesus of Nazareth, who would build God's temple and bear royal honor (Zech. 6:12; John 2:19; Phil. 2:9–11).

Theological Soundings

IMPUTED RIGHTEOUSNESS. The stripping and re-clothing of Joshua in Zechariah 3:4–5 offers the clearest, and certainly one of the most dramatic, depictions of the saving work of Christ in the Old Testament. By the word and working of God, the sinner's guilt is removed. God not only removes the guilt of iniquity; he also provides the righteousness required to stand in his holy presence. This alien righteousness is the righteousness of Jesus Christ, the Son of God, who exchanges his perfect obedience for the sins of his people (2 Cor. 5:21). As the apostle Paul says, "I have suffered the loss of all things and count them as rubbish, in order that I may gain Christ and be found in him, not having a righteousness of my own that comes from the law, but that which comes through faith in Christ, the righteousness from God that depends on faith" (Phil. 3:8–9). This great exchange is at the very heart of the gospel.

> ### Personal Implications

Take time to reflect on the implications of Zechariah 3:1–4:14 for your own life today. Consider what you have learned that might lead you to praise God, repent of sin, and trust in his gracious promises. Write down your reflections under the three headings we have considered and on the passage as a whole.

1. Gospel Glimpses

2. Whole-Bible Connections

3. Theological Soundings

4. Zechariah 3:1–4:14

Take a moment now to thank God for the cleansing blood of Christ, the forgiveness of sins, and a righteousness not your own; and be encouraged, that the good work he has begun in you he will most certainly see to completion on the last day.

Definition

[1] **Satan** – A spiritual being whose name means "accuser." As the leader of all the demonic forces, Satan opposes God's rule and seeks to harm God's people and accuse them of wrongdoing. His power, however, is confined to the bounds that God has set for him, and one day he will be destroyed along with all his demons (Matt. 25:41; Rev. 20:10).

WEEK 6: GOD'S TRIUMPH OVER SIN

Zechariah 5:1–6:15

The Place of the Passage

Will Israel's history be a never-ending cycle of sin, punishment, repentance, and restoration? The final three night visions answer this question with a resounding "No!" Viewing the same spiritual realities from different perspectives, these visions depict God's eradication of sin from among his people and his ultimate triumph over evil and wickedness in this world. Such a message comes to the Israel of Zechariah's day as precious gospel truth, a reminder that the sins and attendant sorrows continuing to plague God's covenant community will one day be destroyed forever. Israel's God will one day reign as King and Lord of the earth in perfect righteousness and justice. The night visions are followed by a prophetic sign-act (Zech. 6:9–15) that serves as a mirror to the opening oracle (1:1–6) and concludes the first major section of the book. In this sign-act, the high priest is symbolically crowned as king, foreshadowing the work of the consummate Priest-King, Jesus Christ.

The Big Picture

God promises to eradicate sin from his people, expel sin from his holy presence, and judge the sins of the nations through the work of his Messiah.

44

Reflection and Discussion

Read through the complete passage for this study, Zechariah 5:1–6:15. Then review the questions below and write your notes on them. (For further background, see the *ESV Study Bible*, pages 1757–1759; available online at www.esvbible.org.)

1. Vision of a Flying Scroll (5:1–4)

In Zechariah 5:1–2, the prophet sees a vision of a highly unusual scroll. The strange features of this scroll contain a message for God's people. What is the significance of the scroll's location, motion, size, and contents?

The angelic messenger first identifies the scroll as "the curse that goes out over the face of the whole land" (v. 3). Then he specifies the objects of God's covenant curse, namely, the thief and the one who swears falsely (v. 4). How are these representative of all covenant breakers? What is their ultimate fate?

2. Vision of a Woman in a Basket (5:5–11)

At the instruction of the interpreting angel, the prophet beholds a basket (or *ephah*; see ESV footnote) going out, and he is told that the basket is "their iniquity in all the land" (v. 6). What does this imply about the present condition of God's people?

Whether the prophet sees an actual woman seated in the basket or a carved image of a woman is debated. In either case, the woman represents wickedness (v. 8). This may refer to the practice of idolatry among God's covenant people or to the related sin of marrying foreign wives (a practice often leading to idolatry; see 1 Kings 11; Ezra 9). What does this vision teach us about the character and danger of idolatry?

With the appearance of the stork-women, the seventh vision goes from peculiar to bizarre. It is unclear why the women's wings are "like the wings of a stork," but what is clear is their destination (v. 11). Where are the stork-women taking the basket, and what is the significance of this destination?

What do the actions of the interpreting angel and the stork-women teach us about God's sovereignty[1] over sin and his plans for dealing with it?

3. Vision of Four Chariots (6:1–8)

How does the eighth vision (6:1–8) build on the message of the first (1:7–17)? What is similar about the characters of these two visions and their actions? What is different?

The prophet sees four chariots emerging from between two bronze mountains, which, according to the angelic interpreter, represent the presence of the "Lord of all the earth" (v. 5). Which two great mountains stand out in Israel's history? How might they represent God's presence?

What did the "north country" represent for ancient Israel? What is the significance of the Lord's Spirit being "at rest in the north country" (v. 8)? How does this serve as an appropriate and comforting culmination of all of the night visions?

----

4. The Coming Priest-King (6:9–15)

How do we see the first glimmers of the fulfillment of Haggai 2:8–9 in the arrival of the exiles from Babylon (Zech. 6:9–11)?

In Zechariah 6:11, the prophet performs a sign-act crowning Joshua the high priest with a royal crown. What does the crowned Joshua symbolize?

"The counsel of peace shall be between them" (v. 13). How does Jesus unite the offices of priest and king (see Hebrews 7)?

_____

_____

_____

_____

_____

_____

This sign-act is related inextricably to the message of the final night vision—the crowning of Joshua is a key part of God's victory over the north country. What does the crowning of a priest as a king teach us about the work of Christ?

_____

_____

_____

_____

_____

_____

Read through the following three sections on *Gospel Glimpses, Whole-Bible Connections*, and *Theological Soundings*. Then take time to consider the *Personal Implications* these sections may have for you.

Gospel Glimpses

SIN REMOVED FOREVER. Every true believer longs to be finally and completely free from sin. This is the hope of the prophet Micah, who says to God, "You will cast all our sins into the depths of the sea" (Mic. 7:19). The vision of the flying scroll (Zech. 5:1–4) teaches us that God will indeed one day eradicate sin from the covenant community in a final and comprehensive way. The vision of the woman in the basket tells us that God will remove sin to a place reserved for his judgment, never again to threaten or harm his covenant people. The psalmist rejoices in this gospel truth with these memorable words: "As far as the east is from the west, so far does [the LORD] remove our transgressions from us" (Ps. 103:12).

TRIUMPH OVER HIS AND OUR ENEMIES. The climactic eighth night vision depicts God's ultimate triumph over the evil forces in this world that threaten and harass his people. Such evil forces take many forms, one of the most common being hostile nations that marginalize, oppress, or persecute God's people. The wonderful gospel message of Zechariah 6:1–8 is that God's people will not have to contend with such oppression forever. God will ultimately triumph over those who oppose both him and those who belong to him (Psalm 2). In the wake of his victory, God will establish his eternal, unshakeable kingdom in righteousness.

Whole-Bible Connections

COVENANT CURSES. The vivid image of God's covenant curse rooting out and destroying covenant breakers reminds the postexilic community that the Mosaic covenant is still in effect (Deut. 28:45). That covenant includes blessings for obedience and curses for disobedience (Leviticus 26; Deuteronomy 28). The blessings and curses of the covenant have many functions; one of their chief purposes is to teach Israel of its need for the one who would bear the curse for their disobedience. Though Jesus never sinned, he nevertheless bore in his body the wrath and curse of God so that those who are united to him by faith might receive God's blessing (1 Pet. 2:24–25). As Paul says, "Christ redeemed us from the curse of the law by becoming a curse for us" (Gal. 3:13).

PRIEST-KING. In the ancient world, it was customary for kings to also function as priests, mediating between their people and their deities. This allowed them to be leaders in both the civic and the religious realms. However, such a priest-king was an impossibility for Israel. For Israel, priests were to come from the line of Levi, kings from the line of David. At times, however, Israel's kings took for themselves priestly prerogatives, usually with disastrous consequences (e.g., 2 Chron. 26:16–22). Zechariah foresees the union of these two offices in the coming Branch, or Messiah. Jesus comes as the King of Israel who will rule and defend his people, but also as the Priest who will offer the perfect atoning sacrifice. The author of Hebrews explains that Jesus can serve as our High Priest because he comes according to a better priestly order, that of Melchizedek (Heb. 5:1–10).

Theological Soundings

SANCTIFICATION. God's triumph over sin begins in this life through his work of sanctification. God's purpose in redeeming a people is to make them—individually and corporately—into a holy people (e.g., Ex. 19:6; John 17:17–19). By his Spirit's working through his Word, God conforms his children into the image of his Son (Rom. 8:29). While this transformation may seem halting or circuitous at times, believers can still have a firm confidence that God is at work in them.

GOD'S SOVEREIGNTY OVER SIN. As we see in Zechariah's vision of the woman in the basket (5:5–9), sin is dangerous. At the same time, we see that God is in complete control over it. Without authoring sin (James 1:13), God is nevertheless sovereign over sin and evil. The evil forces in this world, and even the evil forces in our own hearts, cannot transgress the boundaries established by God (Job 40–41). God is never threatened by the forces of evil and chaos but rather works all things (even the sin and evil) "together for good, for those who are called according to his purpose" (Rom. 8:28; compare Gen. 50:20).

Personal Implications

Take time to reflect on the implications of Zechariah 5:1–6:15 for your own life today. Consider what you have learned that might lead you to praise God, repent of sin, and trust in his gracious promises. Write down your reflections under the three headings we have considered and on the passage as a whole.

1. Gospel Glimpses

2. Whole-Bible Connections

3. Theological Soundings

4. Zechariah 5:1–6:15

> As You Finish This Unit . . .

Take a moment now to reflect on God's triumph at the cross over sin, death, and the devil, and thank him for the ways he is working in you to conform you to the image of Christ.

Definition

[1] **Sovereignty** – Supreme and independent power and authority. Sovereignty over all things is a distinctive attribute of God (1 Tim. 6:15–16). He directs all things to carry out his purposes (Rom. 8:28–29).

Week 7: From Fasting to Feasting

Zechariah 7:1–8:23

The Place of the Passage

Although the Jews have been released from their Babylonian captivity, a remnant has returned to the Land of Promise, and the temple is being rebuilt, there nevertheless remains for God's people a real sense that they are living in exile. They are subject to the Persian Empire and lack a Davidic king on the throne. They continue to experience the painful consequences of their own sin. Israel longs for a final deliverance from difficulties from within and without. In Zechariah 7–8, an envoy from Bethel comes to Jerusalem to inquire about the end of Israel's exile and the rituals that characterize it. As is often the case when questioning God, his people get more than they bargain for. God challenges his people's religiosity and calls them to express true repentance by their care for the poor and needy and vulnerable in their midst. Such challenging words are followed by one of the most glorious depictions of the new heavens and the new earth in the Old Testament. In this, God announces his unwavering commitment to transform Israel's present exilic experience of fasting into a joyful homecoming feast.

The Big Picture

Through the ministry of the rebuilt temple, God will transform the ritual fasts commemorating the destruction of Jerusalem into feasts celebrating the city's transformation into a place where righteousness and justice dwell.

Reflection and Discussion

Read through the complete passage for this study, Zechariah 7:1–8:23. Then review the questions below and write your notes on them. (For further background, see the *ESV Study Bible*, pages 1759–1761; available online at www.esvbible.org.)

1. Question about Fasting (7:1–3)

To "weep and abstain" (from food; v. 3) was to perform mourning rituals[1] commemorating the destruction of the temple. In the year 518 BC, envoys from Bethel visit the priests and the prophets in Jerusalem to ask if the time has come to cease from fasting and mourning. What about Israel's circumstances may have prompted this inquiry?

What is it about the envoys' question that leads them to address it to the priests and the prophets (v. 3)?

2. The Character of True Repentance (7:4–14)

"When you fasted and mourned in the fifth month and in the seventh, for these seventy years, was it for me that you fasted? And when you eat and when you drink, do you not eat for yourselves and drink for yourselves?" (Zech. 7:5–6). With these rhetorical questions, God gets to the real issue facing the postexilic community. What do God's questions reveal about Israel's expressions of repentance and sorrow?

Ritual actions such as fasting and mourning are not wrong in and of themselves (e.g., Ex. 34:28; Est. 4:16), but without true faith and heartfelt obedience, such actions are displeasing to God. According to Zechariah 7:9–10 (compare 8:16–17), what should true sorrow for sin and heartfelt repentance look like?

Zechariah's message that merely external expressions of sorrow are worthless is not unique to him. Earlier prophets rebuked preexilic Israel for the same sin (1 Sam. 15:22; Isa. 1:12–17; Mic. 6:6–8). How did Israel respond to these prophets' rebukes in the past? Why is Zechariah rehearsing Israel's past? What is he inviting the postexilic community to do?

According to Zechariah 7:13–14, what is the consequence of ignoring God's call to obedience? How does this punishment fit the offense?

3. Zion's Glorious Future (8:1–23)

In Zechariah 8:1–3, the Lord expresses his passionate love for and commitment to Jerusalem. He will again reside in his holy city (v. 3), and the city will experience a radical transformation. This transformation is expressed in the city's names. What will the city be called? What do these names indicate about the Lord's purposes for his people?

In Zechariah 8:4–8, the prophet envisions an idyllic future for Jerusalem. What are the characteristics of this renewed Jerusalem? In what ways is it different from the Jerusalem of Zechariah's day?

"But now I will not deal with the remnant of this people as in the former days, declares the LORD of hosts" (Zech. 8:11). In Zechariah 8:10–12, God contrasts his treatment of his people in the days prior to the rebuilding of the temple with his treatment of them in the days following it. How will God's future dealings with his people be different from his past dealings? What role does the temple play in this change?

In Zechariah 8:18–19, God declares that he will transform the fasts of the fourth, fifth, seventh, and tenth months into joyful occasions of feasting. What are God's people called to do in response to God's announcement? How is this related to the announcement?

"Many peoples and strong nations shall come to seek the LORD of hosts in Jerusalem and to entreat the favor of the LORD" (v. 22). Why is it critical for the Jews to be reminded of the universal scope of God's redemption?

Read through the following three sections on *Gospel Glimpses, Whole-Bible Connections*, and *Theological Soundings*. Then take time to consider the *Personal Implications* these sections may have for you.

Gospel Glimpses

FAR AS THE CURSE IS FOUND. So far in Zechariah, God has promised to remove sin (5:5–11) and guilt (3:1–5) from his covenant people. In Zechariah's prophecy of a renewed Jerusalem, God declares his intention to remove another aspect of their fallen existence, namely, the effects of the curse (8:1–8). The image of old men and women sitting in the street is a picture of life free from the curses of the covenant. In this renewed Jerusalem, life will no longer be cut short by wars, violence, or disease. Children will run through the streets unafraid, unthreatened, and unburdened by the worries characterizing life under the curse of sin. The blessings will go to men and women, young and old alike. This picture of a renewed Jerusalem reveals something of the character of resurrection life, a life free from the dehumanizing effects of the curse (Rev. 21:1–4).

ISRAEL'S SECURE FUTURE. What determines Israel's future: her unfaithfulness to God, or God's faithfulness to her? Through Zechariah, the Lord declares that

Israel's future prosperity is secure because he has purposed to make it so and is faithful to do all that he has promised (8:14–15). God's blessings are centered on the temple, which has several functions for Israel. Primarily, however, it teaches them of the Christ, who will tabernacle among his people (John 1:14), offer the once-for-all atoning sacrifice (Heb. 7:27), and mediate between God and man as the perfect High Priest (Heb. 7:15–16). Because Israel's future is secure, they are told not to fear (Zech. 8:15) but to wait with patient obedience for the full revelation of God's blessings.

Whole-Bible Connections

FEASTING. Meals are an important theme in the Bible. The sharing of a meal is an expression of peace and fellowship between the host and his guest. Often, feasts accompany the ratification of covenants, an expression of peace between the two parties (Ex. 24:11). The feasts described in Zechariah 8:19 are not secular occasions. As ritual fasts were observed before God (ideally), so too will Israel's feasts be God-centered. The abundance of food is a sign of the Lord's abundant blessing of his people. However, the table fellowship is more important than the food. Israel's feasts will be celebrated at the invitation of and in the presence of the Lord, a sign of the peace and fellowship God has established with his people. On the night when he was betrayed, Jesus established a covenant meal to be celebrated by his people in remembrance of his broken body and shed blood (Luke 22:19–20). But he established it also in anticipation of the great wedding feast of the lamb, which will be celebrated by the entire company of believers in the presence of their God in all eternity (Rev. 19:7).

Theological Soundings

DANGER OF RELIGIOSITY. Israel is constantly tempted to think that their outward acts of religious devotion are sufficient to secure the Lord's presence and blessing (e.g., 1 Samuel 4). Merely external expressions of faith create a false sense of security, leaving the illusion of God's favor. Jesus rebukes the religious leaders in his day for trusting outward expressions of devotion without attending to the true condition of their hearts (e.g., Matt. 23:23). The Bible affirms external acts of piety and devotion that are in accordance with God's Word, but not when they stand alone. Israel, for example, was commanded to circumcise their boys on the eighth day (Lev. 12:3), but if Israel did not also circumcise their *hearts*, external circumcision was of no value (Deut. 10:16).

LOVE OF GOD, LOVE OF NEIGHBOR. Love for God produces love for those who bear his image. To love a friend is also to love and care for his children. It makes sense, then, that loving God and loving those made in his image stand together as a summary of the entire law of God (Mark 12:30–31). When Zechariah enjoins Israel to love and care for the most vulnerable in their community (7:9–10; 8:16–17), he is not calling for another form of superficial obedience in place of religiosity. Rather, he is calling Israel to express a selfless care for God's image-bearers that is the fruit of genuine love for God.

Personal Implications

Take time to reflect on the implications of Zechariah 7:1–8:23 for your own life today. Consider what you have learned that might lead you to praise God, repent of sin, and trust in his gracious promises. Write down your reflections under the three headings we have considered and on the passage as a whole.

1. Gospel Glimpses

2. Whole-Bible Connections

3. Theological Soundings

4. Zechariah 7:1–8:23

As You Finish This Unit . . .

Take a moment now to thank God for his promises to transform the sorrows of this life into the joys of the life to come.

Definition

[1] **Ritual** – A symbolic action, usually in a religious context.

WEEK 8: THE KING IS COMING

Zechariah 9:1–11:17

The Place of the Passage

Beginning in chapter 9, Zechariah's tone and message shift dramatically. Israel's optimism, hope, and joyful obedience described in chapters 1–8 are replaced in chapters 9–14 by a picture of a people who have returned to their old ways of idolatry, waywardness, and injustice. The mention of faithless shepherds and unfaithful leaders (10:3) and the summons to turn from idolatry and divination (10:2) suggest that the godly leadership of Joshua and Zerubbabel is a thing of the past. This shift has led some to suggest that these chapters were written by an author other than Zechariah. However, the change in tone can be explained equally well, if not better, with reference to a change in circumstance of both prophet and audience. These prophecies probably come from a later period of Zechariah's career (possibly in the early fifth century BC), sometime after the rebuilding of the temple and a change in leadership in Jerusalem.

The Big Picture

God declares that he will come as the King who will shepherd his people with justice and righteousness, protecting and delivering them from oppressors arising from within and without.

> ### Reflection and Discussion

Read through the complete passage for this study, Zechariah 9:1–11:17. Then review the questions below concerning these prophecies and write your notes on them. (For further background, see the *ESV Study Bible*, pages 1761–1766; available online at www.esvbible.org.)

1. The Lord Returns to His Temple (9:1–8)

In verses 1–8, Yahweh declares his coming judgment upon Israel's neighbors and traditional enemies. Moving from north to south, he mentions Hadrach and Damascus (v. 1); Hamath, Tyre and Sidon (v. 2); and the Philistine cities Ashkelon, Gaza, and Ekron (v. 5). What is the significance of these conquests moving from north to south, culminating in the Lord's encamping at his house (i.e., temple) "as a guard, so that none shall march to and fro" (v. 8)?

The prophet declares that Yahweh will overthrow the sources of these nations' pride and security (vv. 1–6). What were these nations trusting in for their security?

In verses 5–7, God declares that he will destroy the Philistines, along with all of their idolatrous practices. Surprisingly, however, the Philistines' future is not hopeless. Zechariah 9:7 introduces an unexpected twist: just as God delivered a remnant of the Jebusites (2 Sam. 24:16–25), a Canaanite clan, from destruction and incorporated them into his people, so too will he bring in a remnant of the

Philistines. How is this a fulfillment of God's covenant promises? How does God's treatment of the Philistines in some ways reflect his treatment of Israel?

2. The Messiah Comes to Zion (9:9–17)

In Zechariah 9:9, the prophet calls Zion and Jerusalem to raise their voices in rejoicing that the messianic King is coming. What is the character of the messianic King as presented in verses 9–13? How would this announcement be an encouragement to the postexilic community?

According to Zechariah 9:10–17, what will the Messiah accomplish when he comes?

3. Promise of a Good Shepherd (10:1–12)

In Zechariah 10:1, the prophet reminds Israel that Baal is not the god of the storm; in fact, it is Yahweh who gives showers of rain to those who ask in faith.

How does biblical religion differ from pagan religion? (You may want to review 1 Kings 18:20–46 to help answer this question.)

"The people wander like sheep; they are afflicted for lack of a shepherd" (10:2). What is the ironic result of seeking the Lord's favor through pagan practices?

In Zechariah 10:3–12, the prophet uses the image of a shepherd to describe Yahweh as the faithful King of Israel. How is an ideal king like a good shepherd? How will God fulfill this role for Israel?

3. God's Judgment on the Wicked Shepherds (11:1–17)

The prophet likens the shepherds of Israel to glorious, strong trees that have fallen and have been ruined and devoured by fire (11:1–3). What message does this send to Israel's leaders?

Prophets were often called to perform sign-acts, dramatic scenes whose actions contained a message for the people (e.g., Isaiah 20; Jer. 13:1–11; Ezekiel 4; Hos. 1:2–11). Although there is some debate about what Zechariah 11:4–17 describes, it seems likely that Zechariah is being called to perform such a sign-act by taking up employment as an actual shepherd. What does Zechariah's sign-act reveal about how Israel's leaders treated the people? What does it teach us about the work of a faithful shepherd?

How do the sheep respond to the faithful shepherd? Is this surprising? Why or why not?

Zechariah's two shepherd staffs are given the names Favor and Union. What do these names symbolize? What does the prophet's breaking these staffs communicate to God's people (vv. 10 and 14)?

Beginning in verse 15, the prophet is commanded to perform another sign-act, that is, taking up the equipment of a foolish shepherd. What does God communicate through this sign-act?

Read through the following three sections on *Gospel Glimpses, Whole-Bible Connections,* and *Theological Soundings*. Then take time to consider the *Personal Implications* these sections may have for you.

Gospel Glimpses

THE DIVINE WARRIOR. Throughout the Bible, God reveals himself as a divine warrior fighting on behalf of his people. He is depicted as strapping on his armor (Isa. 59:17–19), riding his chariot (Ps. 104:3), wielding a sword (Deut. 32:41), and shooting arrows (Hab. 3:9). At times, God employs creation itself as his weapon to defeat his enemies, as he does famously at the exodus. At other times, God uses a people or nation as his instrument of judgment (e.g., Joshua 6). When God appears as the divine warrior, the created order itself responds, often shaking or melting under the awesome presence of its King (e.g., Hab. 3:6). The arrival of the divine warrior appears to induce chaos and threaten human life. However, for God's people, the shaking of creation is a picture of the undoing of a world broken and disordered by sin, serving as the preface to God's reordering of creation under his righteous rule.

BLOOD OF MY COVENANT. Throughout the Bible, formal relationships called covenants are established on oath and attended by sanctions. Covenants were often ratified by the shedding of blood, a visual way for the parties to say, in effect, "So shall my life be shed should I violate my promise." In Zechariah 9:11, Yahweh appeals to the blood of his covenant with Israel as the grounds for their deliverance. This points back to the shedding of blood by Abraham (Gen. 15:7–21) and Moses (Ex. 24:1–8), while also pointing forward to the shed blood of Christ who, on the night in which he was betrayed, said, "This cup that is poured out for you is the new covenant in my blood" (Luke 22:20).

Whole-Bible Connections

TRIUMPHAL ENTRY. The Gospel of Matthew understands Jesus' entry into Jerusalem as a fulfillment of Zechariah's prophecy: "This took place to fulfill what was spoken by the prophet, saying, 'Say to the daughter of Zion, "Behold, your king is coming to you, humble, and mounted on a donkey, on a colt, the foal of a beast of burden"'" (Matt. 21:4–5; compare Zech. 9:9). The people rightly recognize that Jesus comes to Jerusalem as her Messiah (Matt. 21:9). However, they misunderstand the nature of the salvation he brings. Most people mistakenly believe that Jesus comes to deliver Israel from her Roman overlords, when in fact he comes to deliver them from much more powerful enemies, namely, sin, death, and the power of the Devil (Col. 2:13–15).

THE GOOD SHEPHERD. The shepherd serves as a rich metaphor[1] throughout the Bible. On the one hand, the image of a shepherd carries pastoral overtones of one who (ideally) cares for the sheep entrusted to him. This image also carries royal overtones, as kings are often likened to a shepherd (e.g., Ps. 78:70–72). While Israel's kings and leaders are described as shepherds, ultimately it is God who serves as the great shepherd who cares for, guides, and governs his people (Ps. 23:1). Israel's history taught them that they needed a shepherd-king, for without one, "Everyone did what was right in his own eyes" (Judg. 21:25). However, Israel's kings, more often than not, abused the sheep entrusted to them (Ezek. 34:1–10). Even Israel's greatest king, David, the man after God's own heart, committed adultery and murder and sinned such that he brought a plague upon his own people. Israel's past taught them that they desperately needed a good shepherd, one who would have compassion on them (Mark 6:34) and would lay down his own life for his sheep (John 10:11).

Theological Soundings

CHURCH LEADERS. The people of Israel often followed in the footsteps of their corrupt leaders. This is seen most clearly in the monarchy (consider, for instance the reign of Manasseh in 2 Kings 21), but applies to other leaders as well: priests, prophets, judges, and sages. When sin is tolerated or even approved at the highest levels of church leadership, it will undoubtedly harm the congregation in some way (1 Cor. 5:6). Of course, no leader is perfect. It is critical, therefore, that as church leaders pursue holiness in their own lives, they also remind their people that the true head of the church is the perfectly sinless Christ.

Personal Implications

Take time to reflect on the implications of Zechariah 9:1–11:17 for your own life today. Consider what you have learned that might lead you to praise God, repent of sin, and trust in his gracious promises. Write down your reflections under the three headings we have considered and on the passage as a whole.

1. Gospel Glimpses

2. Whole-Bible Connections

3. Theological Soundings

4. Zechariah 9:1–11:17

> **As You Finish This Unit . . .**

Take a moment now to thank God for the Good Shepherd who laid down his life for his sheep, and who, even now, by his Word and Spirit, governs and guides his people unto eternal life.

Definition

[1] **Metaphor** – A figure of speech that draws an analogy between two objects by equating them, even though they are not actually the same thing. An example is Ps 119:105: "Your word is a lamp to my feet and a light to my path."

WEEK 9: THE DAY OF THE LORD

Zechariah 12:1–14:21

▲

In Zechariah's day, life for God's people was difficult, and yet, in his climactic oracle, the prophet tells of even greater difficulties still to come. Zechariah 12–14 describes a future day in which God will once and for all deliver his people from great danger and establish his universal kingship over a newly ordered creation. However, Zechariah's goal in disclosing the future is not to satisfy idle curiosities about the nature of the last days but rather to equip God's people to live faithfully in the present as a people of hope in an age characterized by trial and tribulation.

The Big Picture

God is faithful to protect, purify, and deliver his people as they endure great trials and tribulations by faith.

> ## Reflection and Discussion

Read through the complete passage for this study, Zechariah 12:1–14:21. Then review the questions below and write your notes on them. (For further background, see the *ESV Study Bible*, pages 1766–1770; available online at www.esvbible.org.)

1. The Lord Protects His People (12:1–9)

In Zechariah 12:1, God is identified as "the LORD, who stretched out the heavens and founded the earth and formed the spirit of man within him." How does God's identity as creator engender confidence in his promises of deliverance?

In verses 2–9, God declares that he will transform Jerusalem into his instrument of judgment against the nations. How will Jerusalem be transformed on "that day?" (Hint: Zechariah uses four images in these verses for what Jerusalem will be like.) How does this contrast with Jerusalem's situation in Zechariah's day?

"The LORD will give salvation to the tents of Judah first, that the glory of the house of David and the glory of the inhabitants of Jerusalem may not surpass that of Judah" (Zech. 12:7). What is the significance of God's salvation's reaching Judah before Jerusalem? What lesson might we learn from this as individuals and as churches?

2. The Lord Purifies His People (12:10–13:9)

What will be the result of the Lord's pouring out a "spirit of grace and … mercy" upon his people (vv. 10–14)?

"When they look on me, on him whom they have pierced, they shall mourn for him" (Zech. 12:10). How may Israel be said to have pierced the Lord in Zechariah's day? How is this fulfilled in Jesus (see John 19:37)?

"On that day there shall be a fountain opened for the house of David and the inhabitants of Jerusalem, to cleanse them from sin and uncleanness" (Zech. 13:1). In verses 2–6, how does God describe the purification he will accomplish?

In Zechariah 11:17, God's sword of judgment struck out against the wicked shepherds. In 13:7, however, the sword of God's judgment is leveled against God's shepherd, "the man who stands next to [God]" (v. 7). This results in the scattering of the sheep and a period of hardship and tribulation. According to Zechariah, what will God accomplish by striking the shepherd (13:7–9; compare Matt. 26:31)?

70

3. The Lord Takes His Stand for His People (14:1–15)

While God is going to bring great judgment against Jerusalem in the form of hostile nations, he will also provide an even greater deliverance (vv. 1–5). How does Zechariah depict the Lord's sovereignty over the chaos of this traumatic day?

This climactic battle results in a new world order, described in verses 6–11. What is similar between the old and the new order? What is different? What do you think these differences are meant to teach us about a future new creation?

What is the fate of those who oppose the Lord and his people? Why is this described in such graphic detail?

4. The Whole Earth Shall Worship the Lord (14:16–21)

Not only is the created order transformed; the nations that once came up against Jerusalem for battle are transformed as well. How are these nations changed?

In Zechariah's day, the designation "Holy to the LORD" was reserved for a few items of elevated holiness, used only in the holiest of places (Ex. 28:36–38). However, when the prophet envisions the new heavens and new earth, he sees that such a designation will be placed upon even the most mundane objects used in the most common of places (Zech. 14:20). What does this teach us about the symbolic function of the temple in Zechariah's day? What does it teach us about the character of the new heavens and the new earth?

Read through the following three sections on *Gospel Glimpses*, *Whole-Bible Connections*, and *Theological Soundings*. Then take time to consider the *Personal Implications* these sections may have for you.

Gospel Glimpses

STRIKE THE SHEPHERD. "Strike the shepherd, and the sheep will be scattered; I will turn my hand against the little ones" (Zech. 13:7). This verse describes an unspeakable tragedy. Portrayed as "the man who stands next to me," the shepherd clearly enjoys a special relationship with God himself. Yet he receives the stroke of God's judgment, symbolized by the sword (v. 7). Not only does God turn his hand against his shepherd; he strikes out against his sheep as well. No reason is given for the shepherd's destruction or the sheep's oppression; the focus of Zechariah's oracle, rather, is God's unwavering purpose to work in and through this tragedy to accomplish his redemptive purposes. Through the judgment of his shepherd, God will purify a people for himself and will fulfill his promises of the covenant of grace: "They will call upon my name, and I will answer them. I will say, 'They are my people'; and they will say, 'The LORD is my God'" (13:9).

A SECURE CITY. In Zechariah 14:11, the prophet declares that Jerusalem "shall be inhabited, for there shall never again be a decree of utter destruction. Jerusalem shall dwell in security." In Zechariah's day, Jerusalem was an unwalled city and thus vulnerable to attack from invaders and marauders. Daily life for the postexilic community was marked by deep insecurity, vulnerability, and fear. The prophet, however, declares a coming day in which these burdens will be a thing of the past. When Yahweh visits the world in judgment and salvation, he will establish Jerusalem in never-ending peace and security. Best of all, Israel's eternal security means she will no longer be subject to the covenant curses of God's judgment on account of her disobedience. Jesus bore God's decree of utter destruction against sinners for all who are united to him by faith. Through faith in Christ, believers enjoy a foretaste of that eternal peace and security as they wait for the fullness of its revelation on the last day.

Whole-Bible Connections

STREAMS OF LIVING WATER. Zechariah 13:1 speaks of a "fountain opened for the house of David and the inhabitants of Jerusalem, to cleanse them from sin and uncleanness." Water imagery is used again in 14:8, where we are told that "living waters shall flow out from Jerusalem, half of them to the eastern sea and half of them to the western sea. It shall continue in summer as in winter." A continually flowing stream is associated with sanctuaries, places of God's presence. Such a stream flowed from Eden (Gen. 2:10; compare Ps. 46:4) and will flow again in the new heavens and earth as a symbol of God's abundant and ever-present provision for his people (Rev. 22:1–5). Such provision is found ultimately in Jesus himself, who told the Samaritan woman that he offers "a spring of water welling up to eternal life" (John 4:14). And later in the same Gospel, Jesus declares, "Whoever believes in me, as the Scripture has said, 'Out of his heart will flow rivers of living water'" (John 7:38). The water Jesus offers is his own blood (see John 19:34; 1 John 5:6), which atones for sin and cleanses from all unrighteousness (1 John 1:7–9) and is signified and sealed in baptism.

Theological Soundings

NEW DAY, NEW CREATION. How can anyone describe something that is not of this world, something no one has ever seen or experienced? This is the challenge the prophets face when describing the glory of the new creation. Often, the prophets employ familiar images to describe the unfamiliar world to come. Zechariah depicts the new creation as a day in which there will no longer be day and night, that is, no alternation of light and darkness (14:7). It will be a day in which a stream flows continually from Jerusalem, unaffected by the changing of season or climate (v. 8). Zechariah sees the entire land as a plain, with Jerusalem alone elevated (v. 10). It is important to note that Zechariah is not offering an exact meteorological or geographical description of the new heavens and the new earth. Rather, these vivid images make a theological point. Never-ending light points to the absence of darkness (and dark forces) in this new world. An ever-flowing stream shows God's abundant and ceaseless provision for his people. And the elevation of Jerusalem teaches that the whole world will recognize God for who he is, the exalted and majestic King over the whole world.

Personal Implications

Take time to reflect on the implications of Zechariah 12–14 for your own life today. Consider what you have learned that might lead you to praise God, repent of sin, and trust in his gracious promises. Write down your reflections under the three headings we have considered and on the passage as a whole.

1. Gospel Glimpses

2. Whole-Bible Connections

3. Theological Soundings

4. Zechariah 12:1–14:21

As You Finish This Unit . . .

Take a moment now to ask God for the grace to mourn over sin and to trust more deeply in the sufficiency of Christ's blood to purify from all unrighteousness.

WEEK 10: FORGETTING GOD'S LOVE

Malachi 1:1–2:16

The Place of the Passage

Although the exact dates of his prophetic ministry are unknown, Malachi's oracles clearly address the postexilic community sometime after the rebuilding of the temple in 515 BC. Malachi, whose name means "my servant," speaks to a people who have forgotten the love of God and whose hearts have consequently begun to grow cold in worship and obedience. The book of Malachi consists of a series of prophetic disputations in which the Lord reveals various sins that are spiritually crippling his people, such as halfhearted worship and the fear of man rather than of God. With tremendous rhetorical force, Malachi calls for heartfelt repentance and worship born of a deep and living faith, reminding Israel of the divine promise, "Return to me, and I will return to you" (Mal. 3:7).

The Big Picture

Malachi conveys the disastrous consequences of forgetting the love of God, which he has revealed in his sovereign election of a sinful people.

> ### Reflection and Discussion

Read through the complete passage for this study, Malachi 1:1–2:16. Then review the questions below and write your notes on them. (For further background, see the *ESV Study Bible*, pages 1774–1777; available online at www.esvbible.org.)

1. The Electing Love of Yahweh (1:1–5)

Although God declares his love for Israel, Israel doubts that God has in fact loved them, at least lately (v. 2). What in Israel's past or present might lead them to question God's love? How do we let experiences and circumstances dictate how we view God's favor toward us?

The Lord vindicates his love for his people by appealing to his election of Jacob as the child of the promise over his older twin brother, Esau (vv. 2–3; compare Gen. 25:23). What lesson is Israel to learn from God's election of their forefather Jacob?

How do God's behavior toward Edom in the past and his promises regarding their future reveal the uniqueness of his relationship with Israel? How do we see this same dynamic in the lives of Jacob and Esau?

2. Faithless Priests, Faithful God (1:6–14)

What is the Lord's complaint against Israel's priests (1:6–8), and what does he point to as evidence against them?

Consider verses 6 and 8. What do these human relationships (i.e., father/son, master/servant, governor/citizens) reveal about the depths of the priests' sin? How might we make similar comparisons in our own lives?

What do the priests' offerings reveal about their hearts?

How might these halfhearted expressions of worship be related to Israel's doubting of God's love (vv. 2–5)? How does Malachi's oracle challenge our approach to worship?

"Oh that there were one among you who would shut the doors, that you might not kindle fire on my altar in vain!" (Mal. 1:10). How would a complete closure of the temple and a cessation of worship be better than Israel's persistence in halfhearted worship?

Even though Israel fails to honor God in its worship, God's plan to create worshipers for himself is not thwarted. In Malachi 1:11 the Lord declares, "From the rising of the sun to its setting my name will be great among the nations, and in every place incense will be offered to my name, and a pure offering. For my name will be great among the nations, says the LORD of hosts." How is this a further indictment of Israel? How is this promise fulfilled in the New Testament?

3. My Covenant with Levi (2:1–9)

Read Numbers 6:22–27. What does the Lord mean when he says to the priests, "I will curse your blessings" (Mal. 2:2)?

How does the Lord's treatment of the unfaithful priests reflect their treatment of him?

Because of Phinehas's zeal for the Lord's holiness, the Lord established a "covenant of peace" with him and his descendants as a "covenant of perpetual priesthood" (Num. 25:12–13). Malachi appeals to this covenant (which he calls a "covenant with Levi" in 2:4) to contrast the corrupt priests of his day with the ideal priest promised in that covenant. According to Malachi, what does the ideal priest look like?

How have the priests in Malachi's day corrupted this ideal? What do their abuses of office reveal about what they truly value?

-----

4. Defiled Marriages, Defiled Worship (2:10–16)

Israel was forbidden to marry certain foreigners (Deut. 7:1–5). Yet, judging from Ezra and Nehemiah (Ezra 9; Neh. 13:23–27), this practice was as widespread after the exile as it was before. What does the designation "daughter of a foreign God" (Mal. 2:11) highlight about these foreign wives?

How do such intermarriages disrupt the spiritual life of God's people (v. 13)?

The Lord indicts Israel for a second and corresponding sin: divorcing the wives of their youth (2:14). According to Malachi, what role does God play in marriage covenants?

According to Malachi 2:15–16, what are God's purposes for godly marriages (compare Eph. 5:22–33)?

Read through the following three sections on *Gospel Glimpses, Whole-Bible Connections*, and *Theological Soundings*. Then take time to consider the *Personal Implications* these sections may have for you.

Gospel Glimpses

LOVE OF GOD. When God declares his love for his people (Mal. 1:2), he is referring not to his affection for Israel but rather to his sovereign election of them and his unwavering commitment to his covenant with them. For Israel in Malachi's day (and for us today), God's love is at times difficult to see, believe, or confess. God responds to Israel's doubt with a history lesson: he reminds them of his sovereign election of Jacob and his faithfulness to fulfill his promises to bless the descendants of Jacob despite their sin and rebellion. God's election of Jacob may be contrasted with his cursing of Esau, which is fulfilled in the destruction of Edom. Christians today have a greater privilege as they behold the greater fulfillment of God's promises to the patriarchs and the expression of his unmerited love for sinners when they behold Jesus Christ, the Son of God, who gives "his life as a ransom for many" (Mark 10:45). In the words of the apostle John, "God so loved the world, that he gave his only Son, that whoever believes in him should not perish but have eternal life" (John 3:16).

THE PERFECT PRIEST. In Malachi's day, the postexilic community reveals its contempt for Yahweh by offering sick and lame sacrifices on the altar. Previously, the abysmal failures of Israel's kings pointed Israel to its need for God to provide a righteous and faithful king. In Malachi's day, the moral failures of her priests teach Israel to long for the pure Priest who will offer the perfect once-for-all sacrifice for the sins of his people. Jesus comes not only to offer the perfect sacrifice but in fact to *be* the perfect sacrifice, as he offers up his own body and sheds his own blood for sins he did not commit (Heb. 7:23–28).

81

Whole-Bible Connections

GOD'S GLORY AMONG THE NATIONS. Even though Israel dishonors her covenant Lord, Yahweh announces that his name will be feared among the nations (Mal. 1:11). Tragically, Jesus, the Son of God, receives the ultimate dishonor as he is despised, rejected, and crucified by his own people. As John tells us, "He came to his own, and his own people did not receive him" (John 1:11). However, God's plan is not thwarted. He uses the rejection of his Messiah by a portion of the Jews as the impetus for the gospel's going to the Gentiles, creating one people of God (Rom. 11:25). As the Gospel writer goes on to say, "But to all who did receive him, who believed in his name, he gave the right to become children of God" (John 1:12).

MARRIAGE. Throughout the Bible, the marriage covenant serves as a representation of Yahweh's covenant relationship with his people. Most famously we see this acted out in the prophetic drama of Hosea and Gomer (Hosea 1–3). However, beyond Hosea's sign-act, marriage serves as a controlling image throughout the prophetic books and into the New Testament (e.g., Ezekiel 16; Eph. 5:22–32). Although any violation of God's Word may be construed as a violation of a marriage covenant, Israel's faithlessness is specifically revealed in their intermarriage with foreign pagan wives (e.g., Num. 25:1–9; Ezra 10:18–44). Such unions are evidence of divided loyalties and presage further acts of idolatry and disobedience (1 Kings 11:1–8). The good news of the gospel is that although God's people, like an adulterous wife, are often faithless, God remains the faithful bridegroom who through Jesus Christ pursues, forgives, restores, and purifies his bride, the church (2 Tim. 2:13; Rev. 21:2).

Theological Soundings

ELECTION. Simply put, the doctrine of election states that God saves those whom he has, before the foundation of the world, chosen to save according to his own good pleasure. As Scripture teaches, God's decision to elect is based not on anything *in* the person (e.g., some moral or spiritual quality) or anything *done by* the person (e.g., some quantity of good works); rather, election is based solely on God's free and sovereign decision to redeem particular sinners for himself (Titus 3:4–5). This is a difficult truth for many to accept. Why does God elect some and not others? How is election fair? Addressing these questions, Paul writes, "What shall we say then? Is there injustice on God's part? By no means! For he says to Moses, 'I will have mercy on whom I have mercy, and I will have compassion on whom I have compassion.' So then it depends not on human will or exertion, but on God, who has mercy" (Rom. 9:14–16). Although it is a great mystery in many respects, when studying election it is helpful to consider the intentions of the biblical authors in their discussions of election. One purpose is to instill humility in God's people by reminding them that salvation is of and from God alone (Eph. 2:8). Another purpose is to provide God's people a ground for their assurance of salvation (John 10:25–30). Yet another purpose is to move God's people to a greater love for and worship of the God who would freely set his affection upon such undeserving sinners (Eph. 1:3–14).

Personal Implications

Take time to reflect on the implications of Malachi 1:1–2:16 for your own life today. Consider what you have learned that will lead you to greater praise of the glorious grace of God. Write down your reflections under the three headings we have considered and on the passage as a whole.

1. Gospel Glimpses

2. Whole-Bible Connections

3. Theological Soundings

4. Malachi 1:1–2:16

As You Finish This Unit . . .

Take a moment now to thank God for his sovereign electing love and pray that it would move you to both true humility and daily heartfelt worship.

WEEK 11: THE COMING DAY OF THE LORD

Malachi 2:17–4:6

The Place of the Passage

Many—though not all—in the postexilic community have become cynical toward their covenant Lord. Perhaps in response to the trials and struggles of life after the exile, they begin to question God's justice, his faithfulness to his promises, the benefits of obedience, and the reality of a future judgment. In the final three prophetic disputations, God addresses his people's cynical hearts and reaffirms the realities they have come to doubt. In so doing, God calls his people to a present faithfulness as they await a future "day of the Lord," when their faith will become sight.

The Big Picture

Through his prophet Malachi, God announces that the great and awesome day of the Lord is certainly coming, and on that day he will vindicate both himself and his people through the work of his Messiah.

> ## Reflection and Discussion

Read through the complete passage for this study, Malachi 2:17–4:6. Then review the questions below and write your notes on them. (For further background, see the *ESV Study Bible*, pages 1777–1780; available online at www.esvbible.org.)

1. Questioning God's Justice (2:17–3:5)

The fourth disputation begins with the Lord announcing that he has grown weary of his people's cynical complaints. They say, "Everyone who does evil is good in the sight of the LORD, and he delights in them"; and they ask, "Where is the God of justice?" (2:17). What about their circumstances might have led Israel to complain in this manner?

What are the people implying about God in these statements? What attributes of God have they forgotten?

What does the postexilic community desire God to do? Is this a wrong desire?

It was typical in the ancient world for kings to send a messenger or herald before them to clear the way and prepare the people for their arrival. In Malachi 3, this first messenger is not to be confused with the second messenger, called "the messenger of the covenant." This second messenger is explicitly identified as "the Lord whom you seek" (3:1). What two things will the Lord accomplish upon his arrival as King and Judge? How does this serve as a warning and a promise to the postexilic community?

_____

_____

_____

_____

This passage stands as a warning against a flippant questioning of God's justice or a careless desire for God to hasten his judgment. When the Lord appears in judgment, he will judge completely and indiscriminately so that not a speck of dross will remain among the gold. According to the passage, what hope does Israel have in the face of such a complete judgment?

_____

_____

_____

_____

_____

2. Questioning God's Promises (3:6–12)

"I the LORD do not change; therefore you, O children of Jacob, are not consumed" (Mal. 3:6). How does God's unchangeable character offer Israel solid ground on which their faith and hope can stand?

_____

_____

_____

_____

_____

How has Israel "robbed" God? How might their circumstances have tempted them to do so? What does this teach us about how we should view our own wealth and resources?

_____

_____

_____

_____

_____

What ironic consequences does Israel receive for withholding their tithes (v. 11), and what does the Lord promise if Israel will return to him in faith and obedience (vv. 8–12)? Does God promise us the same things today?

----

3. Questioning the Benefits of Obedience (3:13–4:6)

"You have said, 'It is vain to serve God. What is the profit of our keeping his charge or of walking as in mourning before the LORD of hosts? And now we call the arrogant blessed. Evildoers not only prosper but they put God to the test and they escape'" (Mal. 3:14–15). What accusations against God are implied in the people's complaint? How might their circumstances have led them to conclude that faith and obedience are in vain?

In Malachi 3:16 we meet a (presumably) small group of Israelites who have not grown cynical but fear the Lord amid their difficulties. Although the community at large believes that the Lord does not notice or care about the hardships of his people, God announces that he is in fact keeping a book "of those who feared the LORD and esteemed his name." The Lord promises, "They shall be mine, . . . in the day when I make up my treasured possession, and I will spare them as a man spares his son who serves him" (v. 17). What does this image of a "book of remembrance" teach us about God? How is the book of remembrance God's answer to the complaint and accusation in verses 14–15?

What will be revealed on the "day that is coming" (4:1), and how are God's people to wait for it?

Malachi 4:5 mentions an Elijah figure who will herald the coming of the great and awesome day. This harkens back to the messenger who will "prepare the way before me" (3:1). How will this Elijah figure prepare God's people for the arrival of the day of the Lord? How is this fulfilled in Jesus' day?

Read through the following three sections on *Gospel Glimpses*, *Whole-Bible Connections*, and *Theological Soundings*. Then take time to consider the *Personal Implications* these sections may have for you.

Gospel Glimpses

BOOK OF REMEMBRANCE. It was customary in the ancient world for kings to keep chronicles or records of extraordinary acts of loyalty and service. For example, in Esther 6 we read of King Artaxerxes having such a chronicle read to him, an event that results in the honoring of Mordecai. In Malachi 3:16, God is portrayed as a king who keeps such records of loyalty. On the basis of these records, the Lord will declare of those who are written in this book of life, "they are mine," a variation of the covenant promise that "I will be your God, and you shall be my people" (Jer. 7:23). This image of a book of remembrance written before the Lord (Mal. 3:16) reminds us that the Christian's faith and obedience do not go unnoticed and are not in vain. On the last day, the distinction between the righteous and the wicked will be manifest for all to see, and God's justice and his care for holiness will be vindicated (3:18).

Whole-Bible Connections

BLESSINGS OF OBEDIENCE. The blessings promised to Israel in Malachi 3:10–12 reiterate the terms of the Mosaic covenant. In Deuteronomy 28, God promised Israel blessings for obedience and curses for disobedience. The blessing of a fruitful and prosperous land were, for Israel, a picture of their heavenly inheritance, which would be obtained not through the imperfect obedience of national Israel but through the perfect obedience of the true Israel, Jesus Christ (Rom. 5:17–21; Heb. 11:8–16).

ELIJAH THE PROPHET. Malachi announces that the appearance of Elijah the prophet (Mal. 4:5) will herald the imminent arrival of the day of the Lord. His ministry will be a ministry of reconciliation, vividly described as a turning of "the hearts of fathers to their children and the hearts of children to their fathers" (4:6). Elijah stands as the paradigmatic prophet of the Old Testament. When Jesus' disciples glimpse the glory of the Son of God on the Mount of Transfiguration, they see the resplendent Jesus conversing with Moses and Elijah, who represent the law and the prophets, respectively (Matt. 17:1–8). John the Baptist comes as this Elijah, appearing in the wilderness to proclaim a baptism of repentance for the forgiveness of sins, saying: "After me comes he who is mightier than I, the strap of whose sandals I am not worthy to stoop down and untie. I have baptized you with water, but he will baptize you with the Holy Spirit" (Mark 1:7–8; compare Matt. 11:7–15).

Theological Soundings

THE UNCHANGEABLE GOD. Orthodox Christianity has always affirmed the immutability[1] of God, the belief that God does not change but is "the same yesterday and today and forever" (Heb. 13:8). As the psalmist says of the Lord, "You are the same, and your years have no end" (Ps. 102:27). Speaking through his prophet Malachi, God grounds Israel's hope and assurance in his immutability: "I the LORD do not change; therefore you, O children of Jacob, are not consumed" (Mal. 3:6). The immutability of God undergirds the Christian's confidence that God's Word is reliable and his promise of forgiveness through Christ's atoning death is sure.

VINDICATION OF GOD'S PEOPLE. Though many in this world believe that the Christian's faith and obedience are in vain, the Bible affirms a future vindication of God's people on the last day. On that day, there will be an ultimate and final separation between those who have trusted in Christ and those who have rejected him. The former will enter the blessing of new creation life, while the latter will enter the misery of an eternal death (Mal. 4:1–3; compare Matt. 25:31–46). Then it will be publicly demonstrated that faith in God and in his Christ is not a vain hope or a cosmic delusion. Rather, it is a matter of eternal significance for all people.

Personal Implications

Take time to reflect on the implications of Malachi 2:17–4:6 for your own life today. Consider what you have learned that will lead you to greater praise of the glorious grace of God. Write down your reflections under the three headings we have considered and on the passage as a whole.

1. Gospel Glimpses

2. Whole-Bible Connections

3. Theological Soundings

4. Malachi 2:17–4:6

As You Finish This Unit . . .

Take a moment now to examine your own heart for unfaithfulness and to rest in the blood of your Savior as you await the revelation of the Lord Jesus Christ when he comes again.

Definition

[1] **Immutability** – Pertaining to the unchangeable character, will, and promises of God. One of his distinctive attributes (Mal. 3:6).

WEEK 12: SUMMARY AND CONCLUSION

▲

We conclude our study of Haggai, Zechariah, and Malachi by summarizing the big picture of God's message through the postexilic prophets as a whole. Then we will consider several questions in order to reflect on various *Gospel Glimpses*, *Whole-Bible Connections*, and *Theological Soundings* throughout the entire book.

The Big Picture of Haggai, Zechariah, and Malachi

The joy and optimism surrounding Israel's release from captivity soon fades as the disappointing realities of postexilic life settle in. Israel has passed through the crucible of God's judgment and returned to the Promised Land, but now they are only a tiny remnant of God's people. Their national autonomy is gone; the rebuilt temple lacks its former glory; and Zerubbabel, the scion of David, is not a king but a governor serving under the lordship of the Persian Empire. Even the priesthood, though faithful for a time under Joshua the high priest, eventually degenerates, adopting the corrupt and self-serving practices that characterized Israel's worship prior to the exile. Understandably, many in the postexilic community regard their day as a "day of small things" (Zech. 4:10) and their efforts in obedience to be of little significance. Doubt, complacency, and resignation take root in the hearts of God's people.

Into this context the postexilic prophets, Haggai, Zechariah, and Malachi, come bearing a message of hope. Yes, much has changed for Israel. However, these prophets announce that the most important thing has not changed: Israel's God and his gracious purposes for his people remain the same. God will bless his people, and through them bless the nations. God will one day destroy every evil in this world and every threat to his people. Finally, God will establish his eternal kingship over the entire world, a kingdom comprising men, women, and children of every tongue, tribe, and nation, just as he had promised. As the Lord says to the prophet Malachi, "I the LORD do not change; therefore you, O children of Jacob, are not consumed" (Mal. 3:6). Through powerful oracles, visions, disputations, and sign-acts, the postexilic prophets announce that God is indeed present with his people and will one day display the glory of his presence in a manner never before seen in Israel.

Central to the prophetic message is the coming Messiah. Through the Messiah's sufferings and glory, God will fulfill his promises of judgment and salvation (Luke 24:26–27). While the postexilic temple, kingship, and priesthood are dim shadows of what they had once been, they nevertheless foreshadow clearly the work of Jesus. Jesus will come as the true temple in which God will dwell with his people, and through whom God will be worshiped in Spirit and in truth (John 1:14; 4:21–26). Jesus will come as the perfect priest who, on account of his own moral perfection, will be qualified to offer himself as the final sacrifice for sins. Jesus will come as the righteous King who will shepherd his people in justice and yet lay down his life for his sheep as the stricken shepherd (John 10:14–15). Through types, shadows, promises, and prophecies, Christ is held forth as Israel's hope in the midst of trial.

The message of the postexilic prophets is as relevant today as it was for the postexilic community. Like Israel, who was surrounded by the power and permanence of the Persian Empire, we are constantly confronted with claims to power and permanence heralded by the kingdoms of this world. And yet, like Israel, we too are called to look forward to a heavenly kingdom that cannot be shaken, whose designer and builder is God (Heb. 11:10; 12:28). We are tempted to spiritual lethargy and halfhearted worship, and we need God's uncomfortable word of judgment and warning to uncover our sins. Then we too might respond to his gracious call, "Return to me, and I will return to you" (Mal. 3:7; compare Zech. 1:3). Like Israel, we are tempted to doubt the promises of God, and we have difficulty imagining the glorious future in store for those who trust him. Thus we need to be reminded of God's faithfulness in the past and of his ability to save to the uttermost those whom he has elected.

The postexilic community lived in a time between promise and fulfillment. Israel had experienced God's deliverance in their return from the exile, and yet she awaited an even greater deliverance in the future. Christians today have the privilege of knowing that greater deliverance, accomplished through Jesus' atoning death and resurrection. Nevertheless, we too await God's final deliverance, when Christ will return in glory. Although the new creation has dawned in the resurrection of Jesus, it has not yet been consummated. Therefore we must wait with patience, enduring the sufferings and trials of this life by faith in Christ in the sure hope of the glory yet to be revealed to us (Rom. 8:18). In all these ways and more, we need to hear the message of the postexilic prophets. As he called Israel, so God calls us to remember his faithfulness in the past, to trust his promises in the present, and to look forward to the (second) coming of his Messiah and the consummation of his kingdom.

▶ Gospel Glimpses

The postexilic prophets announce the coming day of the Lord that will bring a great reversal for God's people. No longer will they be weak, oppressed, and subject to the violence of the arrogant and evildoers. Rather, on that day God will grant his people strength, wholeness, and vigor as they share in the Lord's victory over all that opposes his righteous rule. Ultimately, the great day of salvation promised by the postexilic prophets would begin with the advent of Christ, the long-awaited King who would rule his people in righteousness and the final Priest who would offer himself as the atoning sacrifice on behalf of his people. As the apostle Peter writes, "Concerning this salvation, the prophets who prophesied about the grace that was to be yours searched and inquired carefully, inquiring what person or time the Spirit of Christ in them was indicating when he predicted the sufferings of Christ and the subsequent glories" (1 Pet. 1:10–11).

Have Haggai, Zechariah, and Malachi brought new clarity to your understanding of the gospel? How so?

What particular passages or themes in the postexilic prophets have led you to a fresh understanding or deeper grasp of God's grace to us through Jesus?

Whole-Bible Connections

The postexilic prophets develop a number of themes central to Old Testament revelation and anticipate their fuller development in the New Testament. Perhaps chief among them is the temple as the place of God's gracious presence with his people. In Haggai and Zechariah, the figures of Joshua and Zerubbabel serve as pointers to the coming Priest-King, Jesus Christ. Throughout all three of the postexilic prophets, we see God's ancient covenant promises to Abraham, Moses, and David being renewed and, in part, fulfilled in the experience of the postexilic community. Nevertheless, God's covenant promises await their final fulfillment in the coming of Christ and his kingdom.

How has your study of the postexilic prophets filled out your understanding of the biblical storyline of redemption?

Have any themes from Haggai, Zechariah, and Malachi deepened your grasp of the Bible's unity?

What passages or themes have expanded your understanding of the salvation Jesus accomplished for us?

What connections between the postexilic prophets and the New Testament were new to you?

Theological Soundings

The postexilic prophets have much to contribute to Christian theology. Numerous doctrines and themes are developed, clarified, and reinforced throughout Haggai, Zechariah, and Malachi, especially the sovereignty of God, the character of sin, the nature of faith, and the future glorification of God's people.

Has your theology shifted in minor or major ways during the course of studying Haggai, Zechariah, and Malachi? How so?

How has your understanding of the nature and character of God been deepened throughout this study?

What unique contributions do Haggai, Zechariah, and Malachi make toward our understanding of Jesus' character and accomplishments in his life, death, and resurrection?

What, specifically, do the postexilic prophets teach us about the human condition and our need for redemption?

Personal Implications

God gave us the books of Haggai, Zechariah, and Malachi to transform our lives. As you reflect on these books as a whole, what implications do you see for your own life?

What implications for life flow from your reflections on the questions already asked in this week's study concerning *Gospel Glimpses*, *Whole-Bible Connections*, and *Theological Soundings*?

What have you learned in Haggai, Zechariah, and Malachi that might lead you to praise God, turn away from sin, and trust more firmly in his promises?

As You Finish Studying Haggai, Zechariah, and Malachi . . .

We rejoice with you as you finish studying the books of Haggai, Zechariah, and Malachi! May this study become part of your Christian walk of faith, day by day and week by week throughout all your life. Now we would greatly encourage you to study the Word of God on a week-by-week basis. To continue your study of the Bible, we would encourage you to consider other books in the *Knowing the Bible* series, and to visit www.knowingthebibleseries.org.

Lastly, take a moment to look back through this study. Review the notes that you have written, and the things that you have highlighted or underlined. Reflect again on the key themes that the Lord has been teaching you about himself and about his Word. May these things become a treasure for you throughout your life—this we pray in the name of the Father, and the Son, and the Holy Spirit. Amen.